Twelve Steps For Christian Living

Growth in a new way of living

PRINCE OF PEACE PUBLISHING
Burnsville, Minnesota 55337

By the Same Author:

You Can Help with Your Healing
Make Your Illness Count
Breaking Free
Breaking Free Study Guide

Twelve Steps For Christian Living

Library of Congress Catalog Card Number

Bittner, Vernon

Bibliography: p.

ISBN 0-933173-26-1

Printed in the United States of America

PREFACE

Thirty years ago when I reached the depth of depression and felt the only solution to my state of hopelessness was suicide, I discovered the 12 Steps of Alcoholics Anonymous. Even though I was not an alcoholic I found these steps to be a life saver for me.

Because the 12 Steps were so helpful in my recovery, I thought they could also be meaningful in assisting anyone to live a more healthy lifestyle. In fact, with a few revisions I found they contained the basic concepts of the Christian faith, and secretly I suspected that the 12 Steps of AA came directly from the Bible.

The principles of the Christian faith are really very simple, but they are difficult to follow. But then, most profound ideas are simple in nature.

I realize that the 12 Steps for Christian Living are not for everyone. Yet, if people want to grow in their spiritual walk with God, the Steps provide the structure to make that growth happen.

Most Christians are interested in spiritual growth. Yet, most of them lack the tools, the commitment, and the climate to do it. The 12 Steps for Christian Living groups provide this. In my book and accompanying study guide, *You Can Help With Your Healing,* the *process* is spelled out.[1] The key ingredient is commitment, and it is encouraged by the other members in the group who have the

[1]For further information about the book and study guide write to: ICL, Box 22408, Minneapolis, Minnesota 55422.

same goal – the abundant life.

In this book, *12 Steps for Christian Living,* the *content* of these steps is emphasized. I believe that the steps express a theology – or a critical belief system – that can bring about healing and wholeness to those willing to follow it. My intent has been to share with the reader my theological interpretation of each of the Steps. This belief system has evolved over the past thirty years of my own life and as a Christian psychotherapist working with countless others in their search for healing of life's hurts.

Because spiritual growth is a lifelong journey, my belief system, like yours, is ever evolving. What I am sharing is *what* I have come to believe. I hope that it can be a "touch-stone" for your own unfolding and a catalyst for group discussion of the Steps.

At the end of each chapter is an Exercise which helps in the step preparation. The exercise begins with the "Life Example." This example is a dream that was shared with me which illustrates the theme of each step. The dream is used because it is not only a way to listen to God, but more often, it helps us to become aware of the inner parts of ourselves that are hidden. It is one of the keys that can help us to grow in self-awareness, and thus, in our spirituality.

In addition, there are "Scriptures" and "Affirmations" for each step which help us to actively hope for what God wants us to become. These are preceded by the "Life Principle" which is to be verbalized each day during the week of preparation for every step. The "Life Principle" and "Scriptures and Affirmations" are to be used as nourishment for meditation and journaling.

The exercise is concluded with praying daily the prayer at the end of each chapter, or a prayer of our own. Each group participant is encouraged to work this exercise daily to prepare for the group experiences with the appropriate step.

With these "suggested" guidelines offered to nurture your spiritual growth, I pray that you will find this book a helpful tool as you journey through your life with Jesus.

INTRODUCTION

This book is based on the premise that every one of us is powerless in one way or another. There is nothing wrong with this. When we accept our unmanageability, we are admitting to the fact that we are human and not perfect.

Thankfully, we do not have to be perfect. Yet, unless we are able and willing to accept this assertion, we will not be open to change the destructive areas of our lives and, unfortunately, we will not find happiness. Unless we are willing to change, our destructive attitudes and lifestyles will always leave us wanting or missing the mark.

If we do accept the fact that we not only have room for growth, but that almost all of us have the possibility for growth, we will have the opportunity to experience a more meaningful life.

Most people in our society put a great deal of importance on physical health and well-being. This is the way it should be. Yet, everyone will grow old, get sick, and eventually die. Unless we see value in growing spiritually and emotionally we will not be prepared to face those experiences. We will not know the power of possessing a kind of victorious spirit which will make even the difficult events of life meaningful opportunities for growth and maturity, as well as a chance to serve others.

The 12 Steps for Christian Living contain the structure needed to help many people find a more abundant lifestyle. In addition, the sharing in the small groups contains the climate in which participants can express some of their most intimate feelings, needs, and values. Through this process the group members will experience the empathy and support they need. Then they will be able to accept their own situation, have courage to change either themselves or the situation, and possess the discernment to know what they can't change.

A large number of people today spend a great deal of time and money seeking professional counseling. This is important and often necessary to help people develop a more productive lifestyle. Yet, many could get what they need and even prevent a lot of spiritual and emotional, as well as physical difficulties, if they were involved in a 12 Steps for Christian Living growth and support group. Furthermore, my experience as a pastoral counselor and psychotherapist has taught me that *just* getting therapy is not the only answer to resolving destructive living. We didn't get this way overnight, and we are not going to change overnight. Unless therapy is followed up with some kind of ongoing program for support and growth, most of us either revert to old behavior, or we may even develop new ways of acting out negative feelings, ways which are damaging to ourselves or to those we love. Therefore, not only does recovery from destructive behavior require an ongoing structure for growth, but so does any program designed to help us find a closer walk with God.

Recovery or spiritual growth, like healing or transformation, is not an easy task. We need God's help and the help of others. *None*...yes, none of us can do it alone. If we could, we would be God. Besides, none of us are transformed instantly. Accepting our humanness means that we need the help of others as well as God, and this requires patience as well as time. Otherwise it won't happen.

The uniqueness of the 12 Steps for Christian Living is that they are acceptable to all Christian denominations. This is true because they contain the basic concepts of the Christian faith.

This program for spiritual growth and renewal within the church is being used by all Christian persuasions. These Christ-centered 12 Steps unify us all, no matter what our heritage. Just as Christians are united *in, with* and *for* Christ, so do Christians find unity in the 12 Steps for Christian Living.

This program provides an opportunity to make Christ real for those who participate. Not only do they experience His presence through the love, acceptance, and forgiveness of the others present in the group, but they also have the chance to discover the "Christ" within. All that the participants really need is the commitment, opennness, and patience to find Christ in His Word, themselves, and the others present - and then to apply the 12 Steps to their daily living.

Applying these concepts is difficult. It is one thing to know them and something else to incorporate them into our living. This is why our continuing participation in a 12 Steps for Christian Living growth group or some other structured sharing/support group is so important. We need the Christian community. God created us for fellowship, not isolation. Living the Christian life is only difficult if we feel we can do it without the help of God and others.

Christlike living will only become frustrating if we forget that it is a lifelong process. We will never attain perfection. Yet, we must be committed to this quest for the abundant life; otherwise, it will elude us. The healing in our lives results from our willingness to participate in this process and our ability to accept the progress we have made with God's help.

Sometimes the changes are so gradual that we cannot see them ourselves. We need the feedback from others. Because we cannot stand outside of ourselves and see ourselves as we really are, we need the feedback and encouragement of others. This not only affirms our progress, but it confirms the growth made possible through the healing of Christ.

Transformation and change come in stages. Christ not only heals us in layers, but at a pace which allows us to accept and hopefully assimilate that healing.

I personally believe that if He healed us all at once, most of us wouldn't know what to do with it. Evidence of this appears in the lives of many people who are healed or become well physically, but are not well spiritually and emotionally.

An illustration of this point from Scripture is found in the story of the man who was lying by the pool of Bethesda for thirty-eight years (John 5:1-11). He was waiting for someone to put him in the pool so he could be healed. He was really waiting for someone to do it for him. Jesus knew his problem. He really didn't want to be healed totally. He only wanted physical healing. So Jesus healed him physically, but he didn't heal him spiritually and emotionally, because the man didn't want it enough to do his part. As the story continues, the man is stopped by the Jewish authorities. He is told that it is illegal to carry his sleeping mat on the Sabbath. Instead of taking responsibility for this behavior, he wants to blame his action on Jesus. He is healed physically, but has not grown spiritually and emotionally.

Such partial healing is not only true for this man, it is true for many of us as well. Unless we participate in the healing process we will not allow Christ to heal us spiritually and emotionally. This aspect of healing is most important, because this is the only healing we can take with us into eternity. All of us will get sick and die. Yet, nothing can rob us of the spiritual and emotional health. That health gives us the strength and maturity to cope with our physical death, as well as participate in the healing that will help us to experience the abundant life.

THE 12 STEPS FOR CHRISTIAN LIVING LIFESTYLE

Spiritual growth and Christian renewal are impossible outside of the Christian community. This community may exist with one other significant person or with a group of people. Undergirding the 12 Steps for Christian Living groups is the philosophy that spiritual growth happens primarily when we share our spiritual journey with others and allow others to share their journey with us.

When we are willing to disclose our strengths and weaknesses, as well as our victories and failures to others, and when we allow others to do the same to us, we will grow. If we trust this process of sharing, we will find that it will help us to discover more fully the love and grace of God, and also to discover the person God created us to be.

Sharing our story along with working the 12-Step process provides us with the structure and climate for experiencing healing and the transforming love of Jesus Christ.

Following are the 12 Steps for Christian Living[1] as they are compared with the 12 Steps of Alcoholics Anonymous.[2]

[1]As they appear in *Breaking Free*. This is a revision of how they originally appeared in *You Can Help With Your Healing*.

[2]*Alcoholics Anonymous*, Third Edition, copyright 1976, published by A.A. World Service, Inc., New York, pp. 59-60.

THE 12 STEPS COMPARED

AA, ALCOHOLICS ANONYMOUS	CHRISTIAN LIVING
1. We admitted we were powerless over alcohol – that our lives had become unmanageable.	1. We admit our need for God's gift of salvation, that we are powerless over certain areas of our lives and that our lives are at times sinful and unmanageable.
2. Came to believe that a power greater than ourselves could restore us to sanity.	2. We come to believe through the Holy Spirit that a power who came in the person of Jesus Christ and who is greater than ourselves can transform our weaknesses into strengths.
3. Made a decision to turn our will and our lives over to the care of God as we understood Him.	3. We make a decision to turn our will and our lives over to the care of Christ as we understand Him – hoping to understand Him more fully.
4. Made a searching and fearless moral inventory of ourselves.	4. We make a searching and fearless moral inventory of ourselves – both our strengths and our weaknesses.
5. Admitted to God, to ourselves, and to another human being the exact nature of our wrongs.	5. We admit to Christ, to ourselves, and to another human being the exact nature of our sins.
6. Were entirely ready to have God remove all these defects of character.	6. We become entirely ready to have Christ heal all these defects of character that prevent us from having a more spiritual lifestyle.

7. Humbly ask Him to remove our shortcomings.	7. We humbly ask Christ to transform all of our shortcomings.
8. Made a list of all persons we had harmed and became willing to make amends to them all.	8. We make a list of all persons we have harmed and become willing to make amends to them all.
9. Made direct amends to such people wherever possible, except when to do so would injure them or others.	9. We make direct amends to such persons wherever possible, except when to do so would injure them or others.
10. Continued to take personal inventory and when we were wrong promptly admitted it.	10. We continue to take personal inventory and when we are wrong promptly admit it, and when we are right, thank God for the guidance.
11. Sought through prayer and meditation to improve our conscious contact with God as we understood Him, praying only for knowledge of His will for us and the power to carry that out.	11. We seek through prayer and meditation to improve our conscious contact with Jesus Christ as we understand Him, praying for knowledge of His will for us and the power to carry that out.
12. Having had a spiritual awakening as the result of these steps, we tried to carry this message to alcoholics, and to practice these principles in all our affairs.	12. Having experienced a new sense of spirituality as a result of these steps and realizing that this is a gift of God's grace, we are willing to share the message of Christ's love and forgiveness with others and practice these principles for spiritual living in all our affairs.

In times like this, it has become increasingly difficult to define the essence of God — the totality of all of the creative power in the universe. To make God more real to us, history has tended to personify God as a Father. Since God intrinsically is without gender, God can be personified also as a Mother. Therefore the pronouns of HE or SHE are both descriptive because God possesses all of the qualities that are unique to both men and women — since we are all made in the image and likeness of God. In this writing, whenever possible, I will work toward eliminating gender definition in describing God. For purposes of clarity when that is not possible, I will use the pronoun HE.

– The Author

TABLE OF CONTENTS

"...And God saw everything that was made,
and behold, it was good."

Genesis 1:31

STEP ONE

"We admit our need for God's gift of salvation, that we are powerless over certain areas of our lives and that our lives are at times sinful and unmanageable." Step 1[1]

We are in Need of Salvation

The fact that we are in need of salvation is obvious to most of us who espouse the Christian faith. We can easily see that, first of all, we cannot save ourselves. In fact, as Christians, we know that we not only are unable to save ourselves, *but we don't have to be perfect*. God, through Christ, has done this for us. Our past, present, and even future sins have been forgiven through Christ's suffering, death, and resurrection.

Not only are we in need of eternal salvation because we desire to be with God, but we are in need of the fruits of salvation here on earth. They are "love, joy, peace, patience, kindness, goodness, faithfulness, gentleness, self-control..." (Gal. 5:21).

But how do we attain these fruits? This requires a lifestyle, a style of living that is open to the healing power of God.

We all have areas of our lives which are destructive. This is what it means to be human. Because we are not perfect like God, we are in need of His gift to us - to be healed and to be saved eternally.

The 12 Steps for Christian Living provide the kind of structure necessary to make the Christian faith a lifestyle. However, in

[1]Bittner, Vernon, *You Can Help With Your Healing*, Mpls., Augsburg Publishing House, 1979, p. 144.

order for us to experience this life *process* we must admit that we are in need...in need of growth, change, and healing.

There are many people who call themselves Christians, but they have not experienced the benefits of the Christian life. Somehow they have not been able to translate the belief system of Christianity into a way of life. Consequently, they have missed the gift of PEACE that comes from being healed.

The apostle Paul encourages us to "work out our own salvation with fear and trembling" (Phil. 2:12). His plea for us is that we do our part to know the abundant life. Jesus expresses this same desire. In fact, God's purpose in having Jesus be our example is that we would learn from Him to live in such a way that we would "have life, and have it more abundantly" (John 10:10).

God wants us to experience salvation, healing and the abundant life NOW, as well as eternally.

We are

Even though this step uses the word "we," it refers to "I." Each of us needs to say "I am."

At first glance this step appears to be contrary to the way God created us. When He looked over what He had made, He said that it was GOOD!

Because God possessed the qualities of wholeness (both the *male* and *female* qualities) necessary for originating all that exists, each of us is able to say: "I am! God made me, therefore I exist! I am! I am valuable, worthwhile, and a child of God."

Because I am a creation of God, I am loved. God loved me into existence. This makes me worthwhile. I am valuable because I am created in His image.

Because I am the most like God of all His creation, I not only am, but I am worthwhile. I am so valuable that He allowed His son to die for my eternal life, salvation, and healing.

First of all, I AM!

Second, we are POWERLESS. Not completely, though! Because we have value we are able to do many things properly. I have value and so do you. We can achieve many things. Yet, many things are out of our control.

If we really search our own life, we will find that there are many things over which we are powerless. As the saying goes, we are all powerless over death and taxes. Not only are we unable to control things like this, but according to psychology we are unable to control 50-70 percent of what we do and why we do it. Only about 30-50 percent of what we do and think comes from our conscious mind. The rest is the product of our subconscious process.

In the 12 Steps for Christian Living, we do not say, "we were powerless." The implication of this statement is that our powerlessness is past tense, and NOW we are getting it all together.

In my experience, "We are powerless," and we will always be powerless — in some areas of our life. Being powerless is being HUMAN. We will always be in need of healing (salvation). When we find some victory over an area of our life in which we have been powerless, we will always find something else on which to work. Spiritual growth and change is a lifelong process. Healing comes in stages and degrees, never all at once. There are no quick fixes for any of the addictions we may have, nor for spiritual and emotional wholeness. God's gift of salvation (healing) is endless and unending until we meet Him in eternity.

Our Lives are Sinful and Unmanageable

This means that we are unable at times to manage our lives. We are sinful. We not only violate God's laws about loving Him and our neighbor, but about loving ourselves as well. When we do this we find ourselves at odds with God, others or ourselves. We have fallen out of step. We have ceased to call upon the Lord of our life to help us in the process of living.

When we cease to rely on God, we find that we are not managing anything very well. When we are not being the person that God created us to be, the abundant life escapes us.

Sometimes this is hard to realize, because we seem to be getting along okay. We are functioning at home and on the job, as well as socially. Yet, somehow, in our heart of hearts, we know that something is missing. Perhaps we are most aware of it in our relationships to those closest to us, like our spouse, children, in-laws, friends, or family of origin.

When this occurs we must be honest with ourselves. We need to face up to it, swallow our pride, and surrender to the fact that we are powerless without God and may not be able to change an event that has already happened.

Even though this first step seems like a paradox we must accept both sides of our humanity. Certainly we have worth and value because we are a child of God and we are His creation, but we are not perfect.

Just as this step is a paradox, so is life. We not only need to accept our unmanageability and our worth, but also the realization that sometimes the way we win is to surrender.

The first step may sound like a negative statement for the happy Christian who was taught as a child to always be positive and never have any negative feelings. However, it is merely admitting that we are human and that we will *never* be perfect by ourselves. As a result, we need a savior. For the Christian, that person is Jesus Christ, the Son of God.

This step gives us permission to stop trying to achieve perfection and be honest. Step one allows us to be who we are because this is more important than being phony.

Many people, I suspect, have lived their lives for years as I did — wearing a mask. I lived forty percent of my life trying to be perfect. When I felt anger, greed, lust, envy, I would try to deny my feelings and behave as though I were meek, generous, pure, and forgiving. When I was not like Jesus, I would try to act like Him anyway.

I am not Jesus — God's example and God incarnate here on earth. I am a modern person. I am willing and able to make my own decisions about how I want to live. I have my own free will, and sometimes I fail. This makes me realize that I am powerless, and that I sin.

But I must not deny who I am and try to stifle my true self. God wants me to *be* this. That is why He created me. I only need to be honest about my failures and the areas of my life that require His healing (salvation) and my desire to change with Christ's help.

If we can't be perfect and always manage our own lives, then what are we to do? The first step doesn't answer this question, except to say that we don't have to save ourselves or solve this ourselves. *What is important is that God has chosen each of us personally. Step 1 is the beginning of our choosing to live in the decision God in Christ made for us at creation, which means we live in the grace that He has chosen us. We do this by admitting our unmanageability.*

The second step, however, gives us some insight; we see that Christ can transform our weaknesses into strengths, even though we will not attain perfection.

Life Example

Wendy was out walking with her father in her dream. They went to a familiar place where they had walked many times when she was a child. It was a path through a clump of trees from which she had often come home in tears.

Along the path there was an open manhole cover. From this opening, she could see a large stream of water flowing toward a water purification plant. This was the source of the water supply for the city. Her father had often threatened to push her down into the hole and into the water if she would not behave. This threat was used by her father whenever he wanted to manipulate or control her.

During her childhood he had not only verbally and physically abused her, but he had sexually abused her as well. She was terrified of her father and usually did whatever he asked because she did not want to be put down the manhole opening into the tunnel of water.

However, in her recurring dream, she saw herself being placed by her father through the hole down into the water. The water was up over her waist and it was moving toward an opening at the other end.

As she moved along with the water she could hardly wait to get out and away from her father. But, to her dismay, the opening at the end was blocked by iron bars which acted as a siphon to prevent larger objects from getting to the water purification plant.

When she got to the iron gate she tried to make her way back to the manhole to get out. But her father was there holding down the manhole cover so she could not get out.

She was trapped!

What could she do? What could she do?

As we talked about being trapped, she realized that her adult condition of being trapped was different from that as a child. As a child, she had no choice. However, as an adult, she had a choice.

In her present life she realized that even though she was still feeling powerless, there *was* a solution. If she was willing to admit her powerlessness, there was a way out. God could intervene. He could save her because He had sent His son. He could heal her if she would do her part. All she needed to do was admit that she could not save herself and begin to live in the freedom and grace that God had chosen her.

STEP 1

SCRIPTURE AND AFFIRMATION FOR STEP 1

Life Principle: God loves me unconditionally.

Read, meditate, and journal on the following scripture passages. There is one for each day of the week. Then use the corresponding affirmations as daily reminders that God loves you unconditionally, so you will be able to accept your limitation.

Genesis 1:26 — I am, because I exist through God's creative love.

Genesis 1:31 — I am good because I am God's creation.

John 3:16 — Because I am loved, God sent His son to save me.

Phil. 2:12 — God gives me power to overcome my powerlessness when I do my part.

Gal. 5:21 — Admitting who I am makes it possible for me to know salvation NOW.

John 10:10 — God desires that I experience the abundant life.

Isaiah 43:1-7 — God loves me, therefore I can be honest and like myself, even though I am not perfect.

PRAYER

God help me . . . to embrace and accept my unmanageability.

Amen.

STEP TWO

"We come to believe through the Holy Spirit that a power Who came in the person of Jesus Christ and Who is greater than ourselves can transform our weaknesses into strengths."[1]

We Come to Believe

The longer I am involved with the 12 Steps, and more specifically the 12 Steps for Christian Living, the more I am convinced that they contain the basic theology of the Christian faith. In fact, they are a guide for my faith walk. They not only help me to understand the Bible, but they help me to put my faith into practice.

I have always said that unless my faith becomes practical and a way of life, it remains a meaningless concept.

This is the problem with most of our education today. It is not a way of life. It is not practical. It is narrow in scope and advocates looking at only one aspect of life rather than at the *whole* of one's life.

We are a whole person. At least that is the way God created us. To go against this would be to deny who we are. This is why so many people today have destructive, self-defeating behavior. They separate education from life.

Fortunately, today we are at least talking about the person as a whole being. Hopefully, we will continue to progress in this process. Maybe the emphasis of the 12 Steps and the importance of making a value system a lifestyle will help us to change this narrow

[1]Bittner, Vernon, *You Can Help With Your Healing,* Mpls., Augsburg Publishing House, 1979, p. 144.

view of education and life.

This, I think, is what "coming to believe" implies. Belief involves the whole person. It doesn't only tap our logic. It helps us to get in touch with our feelings ... and all of who we are.

Therefore, I see "coming to believe" as a process of growth in awareness of who I believe I am in relationship to God.

This step does not only involve what we think. It involves all of who we are. Often when the emphasis is only on what we think we lose touch of what we feel. In fact, it encourages us to avoid being aware of what we feel.

To have a belief in God involves more than my intellect. It demands my heart and soul. It is a response of the total person to God.

"Coming to believe" also implies that belief is an ongoing process. In the other 12 Step programs, most steps are written in the past tense – inferring that believing has already happened. In the 12 Steps for Christian Living, the word is "come," not "came." The meaning implied here is that believing is an ongoing journey which involves the present and the future as well as the past. It is a process. it cannot be limited in any way – and, especially, it has no ending.

Belief Comes Through the Holy Spirit

All that is worthwhile in life is a gift of God. Not only has God given me what I have and who I am, but also the capacity to transcend logic. God has given me the gift of believing in a divine person who I cannot see. And yet, this person exists and has power to transform my life.

Belief is not something that I can manufacture or create. It has already been created for me and all humankind by God. It is a free gift and it is there for the taking – if I am willing to admit I need it and can't change my life by myself.

Christ Is our Power

Even though we receive the power through Christ to change our lives, He does not do it for us. We must be willing to do our part, Spiritual and emotional growth call for our participation;

otherwise, it won't happen.

As Christians we receive the power from Christ to transform our lives. Not only do we have the example of his life as a style for our living, but we are empowered by his loving presence in our life.

Jesus reminds us that the "Kingdom of God is within," or "in the midst of you" in Luke 17:21. Further on in this same chapter He lets us know that He is talking about His presence.

Christ is WITHIN us. Not only does He empower us to transform our weaknesses into strengths, but He is the epitome of the true person that God created each man and woman to be.

Every one of us has the light of Christ within, and we also have areas of darkness. We have a choice. We can allow the Christ in us to shine forth so that we might be the person God created us to be, or we can be less than God's intention and stay with the darkness.

The difference is whether or not we risk BELIEVING. If we accept this premise, that Christ dwells within us, then we will have the power to transform our lives with Christ's help, and we will allow the "Christ" within us to shine forth. We will *be* what God intended us to be. We will know happiness and the abundant life.

Transformation is Possible with Christ

To use the character traits which God has given in the most positive way, we need to allow the "Christ" in us to come forth. We need to be transformed so that we will be who God created us to be.

Character traits can either be strengths or weaknesses. For example, I have been a vulnerable person the last thirty years of my life. I have been willing to share my story. In most situations this has been one of my strengths. When I tell my story, it encourages others to tell theirs. This process is very helpful, and it is the primary way the 12 Steps for Christian Living groups help people to grow.

Yet, at times this strength has been a weakness for me. Even though it is helpful for me to tell my story, on some occasions this has placed me in situations which have resulted in my being violated emotionally by others. This has caused me a great deal of pain, because I have unknowingly put myself in a position to be victimized.

God wants us to work toward utilizing the character traits that He has given us for the good of ourselves and others. This means that we are to work out our "own salvation (healing) with fear and trembling" (Phil. 2:12). Here Paul reminds us of our opportunity, as well as our responsibility. As Christians, we are to be involved in our own healing and transformation with Christ's help. We are to work toward using our character traits as strengths and not allow them to remain weaknesses or to be turned into weaknesses. For God did not create us with a spirit of weakness, but with a spirit of power and might (II Timothy 1:7).

Insane or Weak

In most of the other 12 Step programs, the word "insane" is used. To be insane means that we are exhibiting a mental disorder. A legal definition for insane is not having the ability to distinguish between right and wrong.

The other 12 Step programs also include the phrase "restore us to sanity." The implication is that once we were sane and now we are not.

There is some truth to this statement, if we consider the story of creation. After God had created humankind He was able to look at it and say it was *very good.* Therefore, originally God's creation was good, but then we were all given a choice, and some of our choices were wrong.

One other ingredient is missing. We as Christians believe in the doctrine of Original Sin. This states that after the Fall we inherited the weaknesses of our ancestors.

These weaknesses are evident in diseases which are passed on, from one generation to another, like diabetes. We may even have a tendency toward obesity or chemical dependency because of our parents. Or we might be prone to depression or schizophrenia, the two most common emotional problems in our society.

For me, being *restored to sanity* doesn't describe the emotional and spiritual process that occurs. First of all, we don't have to be insane to benefit from the 12 Steps for Christ Living as a structure for growth. All we need to be is *human*!

Second, we all entered this world in an imperfect condition, even though God's creation was *good*. Everyone has weaknesses, but everyone is not insane. Furthermore, spiritual and emotional growth will be a lifelong process; we will never find wholeness until we are with God in eternity. We might, on the other hand, find *sanity*, but not wholeness. Some weakness or some issue which makes our life "sinful or unmanageable at times" will always exist.

The second step is often misinterpreted to mean that Christ will do all of the work for us. Perhaps the reason for this wrong interpretation is that most of us would like someone else to do the difficult things for us. God won't do it for us. God in Christ will not transform us unless we are willing to do our part. If change is to happen, we must trust in Him and follow through with what is necessary.

This doesn't mean that God can't perform miracles. It only means that He usually doesn't do it that way. Therefore, Step 2 tells us how it is possible to change our destructive lifestyles. It gives us hope. We must believe that Christ can, with our help, make this change happen. However, transformation requires that I surrender and admit that I can't do it alone. I need Christ who is not only my example and courage, but also the Lord of my life. This acknowledgement is dealt with in Step #3.

Does Christ Transform My Life?

In order to experience transformation and growth, I first have to admit "that there are some areas of my life which are sinful and unmanageable." However, not all of our life may be unmanageable, nor do we have to feel that we are completely without any gifts or abilities. We only have to admit that we can't do it alone. As Christians, we need Christ's help.

In other 12 Step programs the use of the word *restore* instead of transform implies that once we were perfect and can be perfect again.[1] *Transform* indicates that we were not only born with weaknesses, but we won't find wholeness in this life. Wholeness will only

[1]See *Comparison of 12 Steps for Christian Living and Original 12 Step Programs*, pg. 10.

occur when we ultimately dwell with God eternally. Yet, it is something we are all to work toward. Then we will know more fully the abundant life.

Christ's transformation of our lives does not mean that He does it for us. It means that we can't do it without His discernment and help.

Many times we do have difficulty making the right decisions about life situations. We need Christ's help to know what is His will for our life. Yet, many of us have more trouble acting on decisions that are right than we do knowing what is right. To act we need to believe that Christ can give us courage and strength to follow through with constructive behavior, as well as to change our weak destructive behavior into healthy behavior which leads toward wholeness.

GOD DOES NOT DO IT FOR US! We must participate in the process. We must do our part. We need to risk believing that He will help us.

Life Example

One night Mary had a dream in which she found herself on a ladder. The top of the ladder was curved, and it was attached to a long broad plank. She was at the top of the ladder hanging on for dear life, afraid to walk on the plank because she was afraid of heights and also because the plank had no railings. When she looked down from the ladder, she was also afraid. She felt trapped because she was afraid to go back down the steps and also to walk the plank.

As we talked about the dream, she realized that this dream was a description of the way her life was at this time.

The ladder represented her life now. The fact that she was at the top of the ladder was an indication of the progress she had made. To go back down the ladder would be to regress. To walk the plank without rails would be to step out without her security. For her this meant giving up her cigarettes. She had been trying to quit smoking for years and found that she couldn't because she wouldn't.

Significantly, her daughter was at the bottom of the ladder, and she was encouraging her to come back down the ladder. I asked her if her daughter had ever enabled her to keep smoking. She thought a moment and then said, "The last time I went to visit her she said, 'If you need to smoke, Mom, you can. It won't bother us.'"

At the end of the plank she could see her son-in-law telling her that she could make it. Then he showed her how easy it was by walking back and forth on the plank. In real life he had been encouraging her, telling her that she could quit smoking.

I then asked her, "What are you afraid of?"

"I'm afraid that I will get dizzy and fall off the plank." she said.

I told her that I really didn't believe she would fall. The worst thing I thought might happen to her is that she would have to get down on her knees and crawl on all fours to the end of the plank.

"I never want to go slow, I want to run," she said.

"Sometimes we need to crawl before we walk, and walk before we run," I said. She agreed to this truth, but said she still wanted it the other way.

Mary wanted to quit smoking, but she felt trapped and powerless to do anything about it. And yet, she was only powerless if she felt she had to do it by herself.

With Christ's help I don't have to do it by myself. God in Christ can transform my weaknesses into strengths. Coming to believe that a power can transform my life can make it happen . . . if I risk believing.

STEP 2

SCRIPTURE AND AFFIRMATIONS FOR STEP 2

Life Principle: All things are possible with Christ.

Read, meditate, and journal on the following Scripture passages. There is one for each day of the week. Then use the corresponding affirmation as daily reminders that all things are possible with Christ.

Romans 12:1-3 — I believe, therefore I am gifted.
Genesis 1:31 — God said that I am good.
I Corinthians 3:16 — God's spirit dwells in me.
Mark 9:23 — I believe, therefore I can.
Matthew 19:26 — God and I can do it together.
Mark 9:24 — It's okay to believe imperfectly.
Ephesians 1:19-20 — Believing is managing.

PRAYER

Jesus, I believe in your power . . .
and I am expecting to be
transformed.

Amen.

STEP THREE

"We make a decision to turn our will and our lives over to the care of Jesus Christ as we understand Him — hoping to understand Him more fully."[1]

To Decide is to Have Faith

Step 3 is fulfilling the process of choosing *God!* From the beginning of creation, God has chosen us, but the only way that we become His is if we, through faith, turn our will and lives over to Jesus the Christ.

The third step is really a scary process. It means that we become willing to turn all of who we are and everything that we have or will have over to God. We need to do this because we are not able by ourselves to manage our life. We need to surrender and admit we need God.

Most 12 Step programs use "made" as the verb. In the 12 Steps for Christian Living we use "make." Use of the present tense emphasizes that we not only need to make a decision now, but we must be committed to continue making it in the future. We need to do it every day of our lives. This is because spirituality is a lifelong process, and, from time to time, we all backslide in our commitment to Christ.

This step becomes even more difficult when we either question the existence of God, or when our relationship with Jesus the Christ is not what we would like it to be. This may be because of

[1]V. Bittner, *You Can Help With Your Healing,* p. 144.

our limited exposure, our family of origin, our life experience, or our state of maturation.

Many of us who have grown up in the church have developed a "Gi'me God" relationship with our Lord. It is give me this or give me that. Obviously this signifies a rather selfish and immature relationship.

All of a sudden we are expected to do a 180° turnaround and give up everything for God. While growing up, most of us were told that we were to be self-sufficient. Oh, we were taught we might have to call on God once in a while. But then we discover that this is not the way the relationship works. We are not able to handle things all by ourselves, simply by calling on God just when we need Him. Not only do we need to have God a part of our life daily, but we need to experience the Christ in others and in ourselves on a regular basis. We cannot find the abundant life by ourselves, or with a part-time God. We need God and the Christian community.

The first step toward that dual relationship is to turn our wills and lives over to Christ every day. This means that we are committed to allowing the "Christ" within to come forth.

To daily turn our lives over to God demands a decision on our part. Getting to this point in our life is not easy, especially when we have always been in control . . . or at least thought we were. Doing this requires *faith*. It is an act of faith.

Giving our life over to someone we cannot see or touch, someone we do not fully know (not until we are with Him in eternity) is faith. The definition of faith is trusting in someone whose existence can't be logically proven. It is "putting complete confidence in someone or something open to question or suspicion."[1]

I believe that the gift of faith — or the ability to have confidence in someone who is open to question or suspicion — is something God bestows on everyone at creation. Whatever we choose to give our life to is up to us. We all have a god, whether it is the God of all creation or the god of power, control, or things. However, the faith that enables us to turn our will and our life over to Christ is not related to a creed or a theological belief.

[1] *Webster's New Collegiate Dictionary*, 1945.

First of all, faith is a commitment to a person, and that person is Jesus the Christ. As Christians we are followers of Christ. Not only do we believe what he taught, but we see Him as an example and also the Lord of our life.

Second, faith is not static. It is active, relative, relational, evolving, and in the present tense. It has to do with how we see others and ourselves as we relate to our common values and goals. It is always in flux and involves a relationship with God and others. Most of all, faith is in the process of becoming, and it is the element which helps us to respond to what Christ's love constrains us to be . . . his people who live out the Christian life of love and justice.

Faith, finally, is an aspect of the whole person. It is not an isolated part of the person. To decide to turn my will and my life over to God involves all of who I am.

Unless we make a decision by faith to live in grace, the grace that God in Christ has chosen us and is the example for our life, we will never find the abundant life. As Christians, we not only believe this, but we also believe that faith in Christ and commitment to him are necessary for salvation.

Salvation, in terms of the Christian belief system, has two meanings. It refers to the promise of eternal life which occurs in the future, as well as to healing which happens in the present. Therefore, because the Greek word for salvation means healing, this step calls us to turn our will and life over to Christ so that healing will occur. This may be healing of memories, healing of emotional pains, healing of spiritual separation, or this may be a physical healing born out of a decision to turn my life over to Christ.

The act of faith, which results in our decision to throw in our lot with Christ, will cause us to change. In Christian language, it will cause us to become a "new person." The premise is that this will only happen when by faith we risk turning our lives over to Christ.

When we decide to take Step 3 we are choosing to reorganize our relationship with God from a "Gi'me" mode to that of a commitment mode. We are saying that we want Christ to be in charge of our life. We want him to lead and guide us, so that we can become who God created us to be.

Being in Christ's Care

Surrendering to God's will and following the leadership of Christ is a difficult task. When we are used to being in control and even believe we need it for security, we do not give it up easily.

Finally, when we do surrender we may even do it for the wrong reason. Most likely it will be from the frustration of not being able to handle things by ourselves — and then we might be prone to *give it all to God.*

Meaning in life is not found by jumping from one extreme to another. Most often it is somewhere in between. Also, happiness is not discovered in living life that way. It is usually found in compromise and, as Scripture says, in "being moderate in all things." In other words, doing anything to the extreme can lead to sinful and destructive behavior.

We are to turn our will and our life over to Christ, but we are not to give up *being.* God created us with intelligence, ability, and power. He expects us to use these gifts. We are only to turn over to God those things which are beyond our ability to handle; we are to get our will in tune with His.

In addition, He expects us to do our part. Just because He helps us with direction, courage, and discernment doesn't mean He is going to live our life for us. He is not! Unless we have participated in the *faith* process and are willing to do our part after we have made the commitment to Him, the partnership and its fruits won't work.

Christ is willing to work with us. He will be our partner and the Lord of our life. *But* he won't live our life for us. His only desire is that we find happiness and salvation. The main ingredient is His leadership and our participation, not our observation.

God is Still in Charge

Some of us as Christians may feel a little "gun shy" about giving our life over to the care of Christ. Maybe we have endured a lot of pain, abuse or unhappiness. We may feel that God hasn't done a very good job.

The longer I live the more convinced I am that God works for good in all things that happen (Romans 8:28). Even the difficult things in life can have meaning for us, if we choose to see it.

Over thirty years ago I attempted suicide. The period before and after that event was extremely difficult for me. I would never want to experience it again. Yet, it was the event that turned my life around, for I began to see that I had probably been depressed for the first twenty-four years of my life. Now I had a choice. I could either choose to live or die. I am thankful that with the help of Christ I decided to live. But it wasn't an easy process; since that time I have discovered that I had other destructive behaviors.

Turning our lives over to the care of Christ is a daily, lifelong process. What we need to remember is that God is still in charge of the Universe. Then, when things don't go our way, we need to remind ourselves of this.

When Christ is in charge of our lives, ALL IS WELL. It may not look that way at times, but it is. When we take firm hold of this truth we will experience peace even in turmoil. We will know serenity because we have Christ in our life. We may lose everything else, but God is still in charge and Christ is still our brother . . . and in the final analysis this is all we need to experience the abundant life.

To Love God is to Understand God

As we grow in our understanding and love of Christ we will begin to notice a plan for our life. This will be an exciting discovery for us, for it will help us to know God's love for us, and to understand more fully God's love revealed to us in Christ.

Many Christians have wondered about God being loving when they see what happened to His own son. "How could this be an act of love?" they ask. Surely it is for us, because it means our salvation and the assurance it brings that we don't have to be perfect. Ultimately even Christ's death is an expression of God's love, because He raised Jesus from the dead to live eternally.

Ultimately, God is still in charge. To know that helps us to understand God. It helps us to know there was a purpose in our creation and there is a plan for our life.

This step as stated in the 12 Steps for Christian Living uses the word "understand" (present tense) instead of "understood" (past tense). The use of the present tense here indicates that our relationship with Christ is fluid, never static. Not only is our faith in flux, but our understanding of God as He is revealed to us in Christ is also changing; our *past* understanding of Him is changing and our present and future understanding will change as well.

Some days we will feel secure within ourselves, and we will have no problem seeing Christ's love in our life. On other days we will be tired or in emotional or physical pain, and his love will seem hidden.

However, the more we know and understand Christ, the more we will know and experience his love . . . and the easier it will be to turn our will and our life over to him.

To Desire is to Understand

In order to understand more fully the love God reveals to us through Christ we are invited daily to live in the knowledge that God in His graciousness has chosen us. With the knowledge that God chose us even before we were born, we will be enabled to grow in our understanding of the Christ in ourselves and others, and of the Christ who is the Lord of our life. Without this knowledge we will not grow in our understanding of God; our discernment of Him and our relationship with Him will be at a standstill.

Putting our lives into the care of Christ does not mean being controlled by a *punitive parent,* rather it means being in a growing, thriving relationship, not one of oppression, but one of equality and justice. We have a part to play and a voice that is heard.

Prayer and meditation (Step 11) help us understand how Christ works in our lives. Prayer is best defined as desire — desire to know God and His will for our lives as seen through the person of Jesus.

Understanding is also accomplished by being emotionally and spiritually intimate with the important others in our lives, as well as with our 12 Steps for Christian Living Group(s) and the Christian community.

Step 3 is a crucial part of spiritual and emotional growth. Unless we admit that we are powerless in certain areas of our lives

(Step 1) and admit that only God can handle many things in life, we will be very unhappy.

My own life experiences and also my practice as a psychotherapist have convinced me that most of the important problems of life are basically insoluble. They can never be solved, ONLY OUTGROWN. By outgrown, I mean that we must gain a new level of consciousness and UNDERSTANDING.

Often through the process of daily turning my will and life over to Jesus, I discover that the former problems cease to be difficulties or issues. Because of the new understanding they have lost their urgency in my life. No concrete solution emerged, nor did the situation change to relieve the problem. It just FADED AWAY.

Several years ago, I lost a job which I had had for fifteen years. At that time in my life a great deal of my security was based upon financial stability. I didn't know how I would survive without that job and the security it provided. However, in a short time that problem was outgrown. I realized that the only security I would ever have was the security within myself (the Christ within) as I continued to make Jesus the Lord of my life.

When we place our lives in the hands of Christ, we will find that what seemed important at one point in life soon becomes overshadowed by the realization that our most important possession in life is Christ. This happens when we turn our lives over to the care of Christ. We gain a new level of consciousness and understanding, as well as the security to take an honest look at ourselves in Step 4.

Life Example

Bob had lost both of his parents. Each had died within thirty days of the other. As an only child he had been overly dependent on them, as they had been on him. He was so broken by the event that he couldn't function. Even his work seemed overwhelming.

In our conversation his greatest lament was that he wasn't sure they were saved. In our therapy session I told him that I wanted him to record his dreams, because they would help me to help him. This is the account of one of his dreams:

"Mother was in my dream. She was standing in front of a

staircase that was placed between our house and the graveyard. She was happy and smiling and she asked, 'Are you afraid of me?'

'No,' I said, 'but your dead body seems so strange to me. . .'

Then all at once there was beautiful music. I asked her if she could hear it, too, and whether or not it sounded beautiful to her.

'Yes,' she answered, 'we have wonderful music here.' Then I asked her if father was there with her and whether or not he could hear the music as well.

'Not yet,' she said, 'but he will be soon.' "

Then the staircase disappeared and he awakened.

I asked him how he felt about the dream. He was aware that he felt peaceful, because he knew that his parents were with God, and they were happy.

Then I asked him what this said to him about his own life. He said, "Now I know that all I need is Jesus to make my life happy, now and forever!"

STEP 3

SCRIPTURE AND AFFIRMATION FOR STEP 3

Life Principle: Let Go and Let God be God.

Read, meditate, and journal on the following Scripture passages. There is one for each day of the week. Then use the corresponding affirmation as a daily reminder that Christ is in you and you are in his care, when you know that God in Christ has chosen you.

Psalms 6:4 — Being whole is to desire God.
Ephesians 5:14 — Having Christ is to have life.
Matthew 26:39 — Letting go is letting God.
John 4:34 — Deciding to serve God is to be happy.
Colossians 1:9 — Understanding is the beginning of wisdom.
Romans 8:6 — I desire God, therefore I have serenity.
John 6:38 — Happiness is being in Christ's care.

PRAYER

Surrender! Help me to
surrender . . . daily.

Amen.

STEP FOUR

"We make a searching and fearless moral inventory of ourselves — both our strength and weaknesses."[1]

Trust God's Goodness

Step 4 follows very logically on the heels of Step 3. When we have surrendered our life to Christ, we are ready to honestly look at ourselves. We are not only expected to uncover our secrets, but we are asked to unearth our gifts. Without this kind of awareness, spiritual growth would be frustrated.

Trusting the goodness and love God revealed to us in Jesus is an essential element in working the 4th step. Unfortunately, the church has not done as good a job as it could to promote a God of love. Rather, it has taught FEAR. Fear of damnation, fear of nature, fear of self, fear of others, and fear of life in general.

In the New Testament the Greek word most often used by Jesus for "faith" when he talks about healing is TRUST (pisteuein). Jesus reminds people that their "trust has healed" them.

Trust, as it relates to doing the 4th step, is not only a psychological necessity for working this step, but also a spiritual necessity. The only way we will be willing to look at our morality is if we have faith in a loving God. We must have faith that this assertion is true — and the most basic meaning of faith is TRUST.

Growth requires trust! And there is no growth without aware-

[1]Bittner, V., *You Can Help With Your Healing*, p. 144.

ness and no awareness without trust — trust in God's goodness.

In the parable of the talents, Jesus pointed out how important it is not to bury our gifts. We are to be aware of them and expand them; we should not, *out of fear,* bury them. Just as we are to be aware of our limitations by embracing them, and not, out of fear, keep them hidden, so we must face our strengths and not cling to them. Then they will have only a negative influence over our life.

Rather, we need to WELCOME them, both our strengths and our weaknesses. They are God's gift to us at creation. Unfortunately, through life's experiences we have developed distrustful lifestyles.

We must be Fearless

When we are working the 4th Step, we must do it without fear. At first glance, this seems impossible. Especially when fear is so much a part of life, particularly when it relates to how we see ourselves.

Because many of us have too poor a self-image, we have difficulty accepting either our strengths or weaknesses. We have difficulty looking at the positive side because we don't believe we deserve to feel good about ourselves. Somewhere in our past we heard, "Do not think too highly of yourself," or we were taught to be "humble." But humble does not mean being humiliated.

The longer I work with hurting people the more I believe that the greatest fear many people have is of their own DIVINITY. We are told that God created us in His image. God has put His seed in us. This is the Christ within us. Because He put His seed in us, we are to grow in love to the point that we become a "Christ" to others. We must accept that WE ALL HAVE A TOUCH OF THE DIVINE.

We also fear looking at the negative side of ourselves. Many of us were told we had to be perfect or be good all of the time; otherwise we were unacceptable. With this message it is hard to look at our weaknesses. In fact, we are encouraged to deny them and bury them deeper. Then they become ever more negative in our life.

In order to take an honest inventory we must be fearless. We must turn our whole life over to Christ (Step 3). We must believe in Him and His purpose for coming. He brought us eternal salvation, but He also brought us liberation from fear. For the greatest fear is the fear of death, and He conquered it.

Growth without Fear

Soren Kierkegaard once said, "To live is to be anxious." Based on this you could also say that there is no life without fear. This is a truism. Yet, I am convinced that it is possible to take our own inventory without being fearful.

I often say: "Spiritual growth is both exciting and exasperating. Exciting because I continue to discover new things about myself. Exasperating because I haven't arrived."

You will notice I didn't say it was fearful. Fear comes with not knowing a loving God. When we know this love revealed to us in Christ, we can grow without being afraid — and awareness of who we are is a big part of that.

To be able to grow without fear and, more specifically, to make an inventory, we need to do certain things. First, we need to accept that this is not a one-time procedure. In this step the word used is "make" (a moral inventory). In the other 12 Step programs, the word used is "made." This again indicates that the action was in the past and that it could be a one-time event.

To live is to change. As we grow we are often at a better, as well as different place to review our life. This enables us to get in touch with other events and character traits unknown to us in the past. Thus, only doing a 4th Step once is not enough. A better word, then, is "make," implying that a 4th Step inventory can occur in the past, present, and future.

Second, we need to believe that God is both among us and in us, as well as outside of us. If we only believe that God is outside of us, we are limiting the power of God. God is everything and everywhere.

We are able to see this truth more clearly in His son Jesus the Christ, as well as in the sacraments and the healing of the sick. Here the power of God's presence is more recognizable.

To believe in the omnipresence of God and to believe that He is among us will help us overcome our fear. When we come to the realization that Christ, who is God incarnate, is in us and among us, we will feel better about taking our own inventory. If God created us, what we find can't be that bad. It may be that some of the things we have done are distasteful, but who we are is of God.

Third, we must welcome Christ into our lives when we do Step 4. If God in Christ is within us and also among us, we need to accept it. To fight against it won't make Him non-existent. Christ is present anyway, so why not celebrate it. If we affirm His presence, we will affirm ourselves, both our strengths and our weaknesses. Christ is in us whether we want Him to be or not. We can use His presence to learn more about our true selves — the Christ in us who, we hope, will more fully burst forth — and become who God created us to be. Knowing ourselves will help us not to bury the talents and gifts we have. Welcoming Him and celebrating His presence will make it possible to grow without fear.

Fourth, we need to believe God is with us. Even the name Jesus, which in Greek is Emmanuel, means God with us. "They will call him 'Emmanuel', a name which means God with us" (Matthew 1:23).

Growth without fear is possible when we trust that God loves us unconditionally and that He wouldn't reject His own. And we are His.

Taking a Moral Inventory

If we are serious about taking a MORAL inventory, we not only must look at our weaknesses, but also our strengths. When we only focus on what is wrong with ourselves, we have taken an *immoral* inventory. To only look at the negative is being unreasonable as well as dishonest.

Many of us who are involved in spiritual and emotional growth are good at seeing our weaknesses, but we are blind to our strengths.

I remember asking a client of mine to make a list of her strengths and weaknesses before the next session. She came back with a large number of shortcomings and only two assets listed. They were that she was "potty trained" and could "drive a car." The next week, however, she was able to do a better job in writing down her strengths.

Two ways to gain awareness are through talking and writing. The best way to do the 4th step is to write it. Not only is writing a better way to discover who we are, but also why we are the way we are.

The 4th Step inventory is one of the most important tools in gaining self-awareness, because it helps us to discover our hidden parts. When they surface, we need to embrace them as part of us and not reject them. If we don't accept them they will probably surface in destructive behavior or somatic complaints, such as headaches and other stress-related illnesses.

When we think of doing an inventory, we may think of it only as a list of strengths and weaknesses. This is the way I suggest doing it in my book, *You Can Help With Your Healing.* However, since the writing of that book I have discovered that it is more helpful if we can also understand where these character traits come from, why we have them, and what they do for us. This can best be done by working the 4th Step as it is described in Appendix I, which sees the 4th Step as a history.[1]

To only make a list of my strengths and weaknesses seems to be doing only half the job. It is one thing to know my character traits and it is another thing to understand why I have them. Understanding why I am the way I am is an integral part of changing destructive behavior. In addition, knowing why I have certain traits and what they do for me is also important. For if I am getting too many payoffs for destructive behavior I may not want to change it. Making an inventory is a good beginning, but changing those destructive character traits requires an understanding of the roots and also the rewards.

Who we are is a wonderful idea of God. As we grow in awareness we are better prepared to become the "Christ" for others.

As we develop throughout infancy and adolescence, we move through stages until we reach adulthood and our present

[1]See Appendix I, p. 132, *Sample of the 4th Step Inventory Worksheet,* Used by the Institute for Christian Living.

state in life. Who we think we are as adults has been greatly influenced by our past environment and the opinions of others. Therefore, our perception of ourselves might differ from the idea of others and God. What is most important is how God sees us and who He has created us to be. What we must hope for in the 4th Step is that we discover how our view of ourselves disagrees with God's idea of who we are. This can be done by affirming our strengths and being aware of the origin and compensation of our weaknesses — and then using this awareness to consciously ask Christ for His help in transforming our weaknesses into strengths (Step 7).

We who are serious about our Christian formation are in the process of becoming. If we are committed to this then we need to grow in our own awareness, self-acceptance, individuality, and desire to be transformed. When we feel comfortable (not complacent) with ourselves and know ourselves more fully, we are not as easily swayed by the opinions of others. They can neither inflate us with flattery or undermine us with criticism.

When we are unsure of our identity, we are vulnerable to any strong personality that we meet. Our tendency will be to please or to withdraw because we feel threatened. In either case, we will be in a precarious position if we have not grown in self-awareness. When we are working the 4th Step we are aware of ourselves as individuals, and we are better able to grow toward being the persons God created us to be. This means we can think for ourselves and act independently of popular opinion. Then we are able to be committed to what is right and good, rather than what is pleasing and acceptable.

Finally, when we work the 4th Step we are able to be more responsible about our healing and transformation. If we know our strengths and weaknesses we can speed up our "growth in a new way of living." Then we will more readily realize that we are not just a personality with physical and emotional needs. We will be a "Christ" for others and be able to give to others. We will be the person God created us to be. We will be "the light of the world." (Matthew 5:14)

Life Example

I remember working with a very sensitive young man. He had been raised in the church but had fallen away. For him, the church had presented an oppressive view of life.

In the dream, he awoke at dawn. The day was beautiful, and he had the feeling that this was going to be an important day. He left his house because he knew he had to go.

After he was out of the house, he suddenly realized that he had to return. The thought filled him with anxiety and fear. As he approached the door, a feeling of dread came over him, because he knew he would have to see his father. He knew this would be painful. His father also felt uncomfortable about the encounter.

As the son reached the door, he could see that his father was in great pain, but he stepped aside to let his son enter. His father's eyes resembled those of a weeping boy. The son realized that there was nothing he could do for his father. He would have to cry alone.

When the son entered the house, he found his younger brothers and sisters waiting for him. They seemed to be waiting to see what he would do when he saw his father cry. At the sight of their brother they laughed and happily gathered around him. It was as if an evil spell had been broken. They began to jump and dance. He took them all into his arms. Finally he led them outside toward the house of a beautiful young woman. Then the dreamer awakened.

This dream was the vehicle by which this young man became aware of his strengths and weaknesses. One of his weaknesses was his own lack of personal authority and individuality. His life seemed to be one rebellion after another, against his father.

In the dream he realized that the key to resolving this issue was to confront his father. If he would face his father, he would find hope and direction for his life.

His dream was a description of the image he had of his father and his feelings of never having been accepted by him. This, however, is not necessarily the true image of the father, yet, this is the way he was portrayed in the dream.

In the dream the father represented an uncaring person. Through the dream the son also had to face his own resentment that had turned to apathy and indifference. He had to care about his own inner sickness if he was going to find a happiness in his life and be able to be independent of his father.

Also, this dream helped the son to have hope. It began as he was on his way to see a young woman. This indicated that he could find a life of his own and be his own person.

The insights that this man gained helped him to decide to drop out of college. He was there for the wrong reason, to please his father. He now realized that he was an individual who could direct his own life. Through this awareness he discovered his weakness. He had to deal with his father.

He also discovered his strength. He was able to face his father. Finally, through this revealing dream, he also experienced direction for his life, because he understood where his lack of authority originated.

STEP 4

SCRIPTURES AND AFFIRMATION FOR STEP 4

Life Principle: No growth without awareness.

Read, meditate, and journal on the following Scripture passages. There is one for each day of the week. Then use the corresponding affirmation as a daily reminder that we need to know ourselves.

I John 4:18	— Love has no room for fear.
Hebrews 2:14-15	— With Jesus there is no fear.
John 17:21-22	— We are one with Christ.
Ephesians 4:7	— We are God's gift.
II Timothy 3:16	— I will affirm awareness.
Galatians 5:19-23	— God's will is my will.
Luke 17:21	— I am becoming a "Christ" for others.

PRAYER

Lord, help me to embrace and celebrate my own awareness.

Amen.

STEP FIVE

"We admit to Christ, to ourselves, and to another human being the exact nature of our sins."

Sin is . . . NOT Confessing

Step 4 has prepared us to be able to say out loud to another person not only our strengths and weaknesses, but also how we have become what we are and all that we are presently in process of becoming. So Step 5 is a confession.

When we think of confession, we most often think of sin. Step 5 is a confession of sin, but it is much more than that. It is also a self-disclosure of who we are. It is an exercise in self-awareness.

The sinful part of life has often been defined as that behavior or attitude which separates us from Christ, others and even ourselves. This could be neglecting to admit either our weaknesses or our strengths. It can be just as sinful to withhold our weaknesses as it could be to veil our strengths.

Nothing separates us from the rest of the world more than our need to LOOK GOOD...or our need to LOOK BAD. When we are dishonest about ourselves we cut ourselves off from others as well as ourselves. We build a wall around ourselves and we can neither embrace ourselves with love nor receive love from others. We are an island, and we are feeling alone and rejected.

We behave like this because we are afraid we will not be accepted for who we are. We fear that our weaknesses will be much too bad and our strengths will not be good enough.

We are afraid of rejection, so we choose deception. Usually, though, we are more into self-deception. When we allow our fear to cover up who we are rather than push us toward disclosure, we set ourselves up for the very thing we do not want — REJECTION.

Because we anticipate not being accepted, our exposure about ourselves is incomplete. We think we will be endeared to people if we play down our sin of thought, word, and deed. In the same way we might even minimize our strengths in hopes that others might be less judgmental about our irresponsibility.

Before we know it we have isolated ourselves by our unwillingness to be truthful. *Nothing draws us to others or others to us like honesty.*

When we admit our humanity, we are admitting that we are both saint and sinner. We are acknowledging where we have been destructive with our lives as well as declaring our God-given abilities to live a responsible life.

Confession is the beginning of changing sinful attitudes and destructive behavior because it is an admission of *both* our weaknesses and our strengths.

Nothing Changes without Confession

Confessing our sin does not give us control over it, but confession does give us an opportunity to have power over it. When we are willing to NAME the unmanageable areas of our lives, we have power over them.

In Genesis 2:19 God gives humankind power over the animals by allowing them to give animals names. Through the gift of allowing us to name things God gave us power to be in charge of the rest of creation, as well as our own lives.

Confessing our sin is NAMING our sin. Admitting our destructive attitudes and behaviors allows Christ's transforming power to be activated in our lives to change our weaknesses into strengths.

However, change is difficult when we don't expose our strengths. Even though confession of sin is very commendable, it alone does not give us power over our weaknesses. We also need to name our strengths. Otherwise, we could be *stuck*, feeling we are lacking the resources to change.

When we disclose our strengths, we are owning the gifts that God has given to us. We are not helpless. We have qualities that will be useful in our healing and transforming process.

These strengths, however, are useless unless we acknowledge them. It is not enough to internalize our positive character traits. We must bring them to light by talking about them. If we don't own them we may not even know we have them, and if they are not uncovered we will not be able to use them to change.

Confession is Choosing Honesty and not Perfection

Attempting to follow the ethics of Jesus perfectly will result in failure. The expectations that Jesus expressed in the Sermon on the Mount reach beyond the ability of most of us. No matter how hard we work at loving and forgiving, we do not do it perfectly. We try and fail, and try and fail again. Our striving to be perfect can at times produce discouragement.

What is the answer? In John 3:16, Jesus reminds us that God loves us unconditionally, in spite of our imperfection. In the Great Commandment, Jesus tells us that in response to this we are to love God, our neighbor and ourselves (Matthew 22:37-39).

In our desire to be perfect we sometimes forget that we are also to love ourselves. This, too, is Christ-like love. Many of us have failed to include ourselves in the group of persons who we are to love responsibly.

To be responsible to ourselves implies that we are to love ourselves as God loves us. Because God's love is unconditional, we are to love ourselves even though we are not perfect. We are to accept EVEN our sins and admit them, as well as our good deeds and affirm ourselves for them.

At this point we begin to see that honesty is more important to God, self, and others than perfection. Since we have difficulty being perfect, God expects us to be truthful. This does not mean that we do not work at being the best person we know how to be, nor that we minimize our strengths. It only means that we love ourselves enough to accept our weaknesses and our strengths. One of the greatest virtues then is honesty.

Confession allows us to be honest and accept ourselves, even our imperfections. Confession empowers us to follow Jesus' commandment to love our neighbor as we love ourselves. This commandment assumes a healthy self-love. The best way we can love ourselves is to name our weaknesses and our strengths, for this gives us the ability to enlist Christ's power to transform our weaknesses into strengths (Steps 6 and 7).

Psychologists tell us that depression is most likely to occur among those who set impossible standards. When these are not achieved, the person is left with guilt and self-hatred. Conscientious Christians are prime candidates for depression. (Depression is usually anger focused at oneself.)

Unless we, as Christians, are honest enough to admit that we don't do all that God asks us to do, we will get into the cycle of trying to do the impossible and then hating ourselves for failing. Similarly, we will dislike ourselves if we don't acknowledge the good that we do.

Just facing up to the reality and admitting to God, ourselves, and another person that we are not and have not been perfect is a relief. Confession allows us to be at peace with ourselves, because we know that our salvation is not dependent on our perfection, but more so on our honesty. Honesty enables us to be forgiven, and honesty affirms the abilities God has given us to be the most responsible person we can be.

Confession is Not Denying

Many people continue in their destructive attitudes and neglect to use the strengths they have through denial. Confession helps us to get beyond denial.

The most common way we deny our strengths and weaknesses is to use the excuse that we don't know how to talk about them. We say we can't verbalize our unmanageability, because we don't know how to express it. "It is unclear," we say. Conversely, we fear our strengths might be seen as bragging; therefore, at times we minimize them under the guise of being humble. We deceive ourselves with this line of thinking, because most often clarity comes with talking. Many of us don't know how to talk about something until we start talking.

I have been a perfectionist a great deal of my life. Some time ago I concluded that it is more important to be the person God created me to be than to be perfect. The reason for this is that I believe God's will for my life is to be myself and not to be sinless. If He thought we could live without sin, He would not have sent His "only begotten Son" to die for our sins, and if God had created us without abilities He wouldn't have expected us to follow the example of Jesus.

God's primary expectation is that we work toward living the best kind of life we can, then be honest enough to admit when we don't and be grateful enough to thank Him when we do.

When we don't confess our strengths and weaknesses we deny them. Denial leads to forgetfulness, and forgetfulness results in being stuck in destructive living. Being forgetful leads to powerlessness and cyclic unproductive behavior.

Unfortunately, forgetfulness, just like our inability to clarify what we need to say, becomes a common excuse many of us use to be dishonest. Confession could eliminate all of this and could prevent us from denying our abilities and failures. When we name them we have power to turn our life around. Denial robs us of our power to change what needs to be changed and use the gifts we have in the best way possible.

Confession is Changing Attitudes

Confession initiates the possibility of changing our attitudes.

When we become aware of sin in our life, our first inclination is to want to change the outward behavior. Such change is important and often necessary to alter our attitudes. Yet, the key to transforming destructive behavior is adjusting how we think.

Without destructive thoughts there would not be destructive behavior. In the Sermon on the Mount (Matthew 5-7) Jesus emphasizes that the thought is as bad as the deed. He pointed out that we need to focus on our inner condition. We cannot live in denial of what is going on inside such as anger, guilt, fear, lust, or envy. Confession is the way to name these destructive attitudes. When we do this we have the power with Christ's help to change them (Step 6).

We also need to confess our positive attitudes such as hope, patience, love, joy, and faithfulness. These good thoughts can give us the power to overcome those that are negative. In addition, owning our strengths encourages us to take responsibility for our own lives instead of leaving it all up to God.

We need to acknowledge both the negative and positive attitudes. Otherwise, we will remain stuck and be unable to use our healthy thoughts to overcome our unhealthy ones.

Confession is the Key to Serenity

We live in a culture which is opposed to serenity. There are no rewards for inner peace. Our society encourages compulsivity, competition and workaholism. It advocates power and control and does not care how it is attained.

Thus, we are a society of CLINGERS. We hang on to control and power. Not only is this true in secular society, but it is true in the field of religion as well. Even though we have made great strides in ecumenism, we still have a ways to go. Most denominations and even individual parishes are still out to protect THEIR turf. They want the power that comes with numbers and flashy buildings. This is not necessarily wrong, but it should not be our primary value.

Confession could first be a deterrent to the sin of CLINGING. Confession can help us to begin to *let go of those destructive attitudes* that cause us to become the addictive society that we are. It can also help us to affirm our power so that we might assume more responsibility for clarifying our values and living a more abundant life.

Letting go of *things* is not enough, however. Confession helps us to let go of destructive attitudes toward things. Spirituality is more than letting go of things; it requires letting go of attitudes — the attitudes that result in addiction because we don't want to acknowledge our strengths or weaknesses. Confession can help us do this.

Second, in addition to release from this sin of clinging, confession can also help us let go of the sin of PROJECTION. Projection is not allowing others to be who they are. When we are immature many of us have difficulty in letting others be different or be themselves. Some might think that this is advocating permissiveness. That is the extreme of letting people be. We need to find the middle ground between projection and permissiveness. This can best be obtained when we admit both our weaknesses and our strengths. Perhaps we most often get into projection when we feel inadequate, and this may result mainly from the unwillingness to admit our strengths. When we are dissatisfied with ourselves we try to put our ways and attitudes on others. By this I am not saying we don't have a right to express our values, but we need to do it without expectations that others will do what we say.

Confession is a way to help us let go of others. It can help us to expose our negative feelings as well as our positive feelings about ourselves, thereby being in a better position to see ourselves as we REALLY are.

Third, confession can help us LET SIN BE SIN for a while. At times many of us would like to ignore the fact that we have sin. In fact, there are people in our society who wish they could eliminate this word. Even a famous psychiatrist, Karl Menninger, wrote a book entitled, *Whatever Became of Sin.* He, too, thought that the denial of sin was not only odd, but destructive.

At the same time we need to own our strengths in order to let sin be sin. If we are only aware of what is wrong with our lives, we may have difficulty admitting our shortcomings. However, when we recognize that we have both *strengths* and weaknesses this task becomes easier.

When we confess both our assets and our liabilities, then the unmasking of our sin can be an instructive element in our lives and in the lives of others.

Fourth, confession can help us to allow PAIN TO BE PAIN. When we refuse to admit the emotional and spiritual pain in our lives we are not able to *listen* to it. Pain has something to say to us. It is telling us that something is wrong or isn't working. This is not only true of psychospiritual pain, but physical pain as well.

When we deny it, or don't confess it out loud to someone else, we are not able to learn from it. Not confessing it or allowing pain to be pain will not only cause us more pain, but this denial could get in the way of our healing.

Confession helps us to let pain be pain and enables the salvation and healing process to occur.

In a similar way, we need to allow JOY TO BE JOY. We need to listen to the good in our lives as well. Unless we do, we will not know what we need to do to continue to experience more fully the abundant life.

Confession is Ongoing

Many of us feel that once we have worked the 5th Step, we don't have to do it again. Wrong! Confessing our shortcomings as well as our giftedness to Christ, ourself, and one other person is a lifelong process.

We change daily whether we want to or not. What this means is that we continue to admit all that we are continuing to discover about who we are to Christ, to ourself, and to one other person.

The process involved in our continuing to confess is fourfold. First, we need awareness. Our sensitivity to those things that bother us and affirm us must grow, and we must *not* deny them. Remember, if nothing ever bothers us, then we most certainly are not doing any growing. Conversely, if we never know any serenity, we are not changing what needs to be changed.

Second, we need to accept the reality that a part of us exists which is supporting discomfort or serenity. In other words, we wouldn't feel this twinge of conscience if there weren't some conflict with our values. By the same token, we would not be at peace with our lives if we were not being faithful to our values. We need to listen to what is going on inside. This can best be done by doing a 5th Step.

Third, we need to call upon the "Christ" within to give us the courage we need to own our strengths and weakness. Through confession we can formulate the *why* of what is going on inside. Then it is more possible to find a solution or continue doing what is working. Through the process of confession we can grow in understanding. When we stop denying we are able to discover the "Christ" within and experience more fully the fulfilling life.

Fourth, after confessing we need to use the assets we have to fill the vacuum left by admitting our shortcomings. We need to replace them with positive attitudes and behaviors. This must be based on what we know to be the true values of our Christian faith, as well as what we ourselves value.

This last part of the confession process prepares us for Step 6 and subsequently Step 7. Unless we begin to change our destructive attitudes and behavior by using the gifts God has given us, we will probably revert back to the unhealthy ones, or to something even worse (Luke 11:24-26).

Life Example

Joyce felt that her growing process was stalled. For some time I had encouraged her to record her dreams. She had been resisting it because she was afraid of what she would discover. That night after our session she had a dream and she recorded it.

She found herself alone in a desert. It was midday. The sun was high over her head. It was extremely hot. Suddenly she heard a voice. It seemed as though it was coming out of the bright light of the sun.

"Your pride, Joyce, your pride . . . let go of it," were the words she heard. At that point she awakened.

When we talked about it at our next meeting she knew exactly what the dream was telling her. She was in a desert, spiritually, and her pride was getting in her way.

We talked about her pride . . . her pride of not being willing to admit that she was also wrong in the relationship with her husband. As we discussed this she discovered that her unwillingness to admit her part of the problem was due to her inability to affirm the many strengths that she had.

She did her 5th Step with me that day. She confessed her weaknesses and strengths. It is true that sometimes we can take care of our confession in therapy. But we need to remember that confession isn't necessarily therapy, and therapy may *not* mean working the 5th Step. However, for Joyce it was.

STEP 5

SCRIPTURE AND AFFIRMATION FOR STEP 5

Life Principle: Let sin *be* sin and joy *be* joy by admitting it.

Read, meditate, and journal on the following Scripture passages. There is one for each day of the week. Then use the corresponding affirmation as a daily reminder that God's love is unconditional and that confession is a necessary step toward transformation.

Psalm 32:5	— I will confess my sin and experience forgiveness.
Genesis 2:19	— God's power is found through confession.
I John 1:9	— Confession equals serenity.
Isaiah 1:18	— Admitting my sin will clean up my act.
Psalm 51:6	— Honesty is the beginning of wisdom.
James 5:16	— I will confess my sin and I will be healed.
Luke 11:24-25	— When I am emptied of sin I will be filled with love, joy, peace, and forgiveness.

PRAYER

God, thank you for confession and the willingness to be honest.

Amen.

STEP SIX

"We become entirely ready to have Christ heal all these defects of character that prevent us from having a more spiritual lifestyle."[1]

Don't Lose the Enthusiasm

Now that we have emptied ourselves by working Step 5 we are ready to be filled with new attitudes and new behaviors. This step naturally follows Step 5 for this reason. Not only are we now ENTIRELY READY, but we are probably feeling more than ever the love of God. God's love has been shown to us in such a powerful way through the "Christ" we have experienced in our confessor.

This motivation that comes from having experienced the love of Christ through confession is an important and necessary part of the healing process. Without it we would easily revert back to old attitudes and behavior, or as Luke 11:24-26 reminds us, we could be worse off than we were before. We need to begin working on our healing immediately.

This is the one step about which we need to be compulsive. Otherwise, we will not take advantage of the momentum we have gained through confession. We need to act on our newfound serenity and peace, knowing that we will realize even more joy as we experience the process of healing.

[1]V. Bittner, *Breaking Free*, p. 123. This step was changed from the original writing of these steps found in *You Can Help With Your Healing*, p. 144.

The Key to Spirituality

Step 6 is the key to our movement toward spiritual growth. Most of us who have come from the Christian tradition believe that the fall of man/woman was a fall from perfection, which implies that spirituality means becoming more perfect.

As I have grown in my own spirituality, I realize that this is really the wrong premise. None of us can attain perfection by ourselves. We are only able to do that through the forgiveness of Christ.

However, with Christ's help we can attain a desire for healing, growth and transformation.

St. Irenaeus believes this, too. Spirituality is not the pursuit of perfection. Rather, it is the pursuit of growth. For Irenaeus, the Fall is not a fall from perfection, but a frustration of growth.

If this is true, and I believe it is, then our greatest sin is that we are not ENTIRELY READY. This is not only the sin of those of us who pursue spirituality, but the sin of the church as well.

Often I am called upon to lead retreats on spirituality, both by laity and clergy. This is the cry of the church today. Its members are hungry, hungry to grow spiritually. When clergy are asked what they want most, they respond by saying they want to grow spiritually.

Why? Perhaps our inner voice, which is the "Christ" within, knows what we need most. We need to be ready to grow.

Interestingly, both clergy and laity often do not avail themselves of this opportunity, because all of us alike are suffering from the greatest sin of all — the sin of the fall. WE ARE NOT ENTIRELY READY.

I am convinced that the way we grow spiritually is not by "removing our shortcomings." This is a perfection model or a "be perfect theology." It is impossible!

Perfection is not something we can achieve or can do anything about through our own power, *but growth* is. We can do our part in *growing,* but not in being perfect.

In the 12 Steps for Christian Living we have eliminated the word "remove," and replaced it with "heal."

I could not believe that God would want us to be something other than what He created us to be . He wants us to be our *true* selves. He wants us to be healed of sinful attitudes and freed of destructive behaviors.

God wants us to reach our potential for growth, which we lost at the Fall. He wants us to be *free* to grow equally through Joy and pain, as well as through sin and forgiveness. To do this we have to be "entirely ready."

Being "entirely ready" is somewhat of a paradox. It is true that this is necessary for Christ's healing to take place. Yet, sometimes we will not be entirely ready until we experience healing . . . the healing of our past memories.

However, if we will allow Christ's healing to take place, then we will be ready for Step 7, to have Christ transform our behavior.

Become Ready for Christ's Healing

In the 12 Steps for Christian Living we use the words *become, Christ's,* and *heal,* instead of *were, God,* and *remove,* which are found in the other 12 step programs. I want to deal with each one of these differences in detail.

First, our use of *become* instead of *were.* Because the 12 Steps are a lifestyle, they are a structure for spiritual growth that needs to be used daily. Unless our Christian faith becomes practical (applied to daily living) it is meaningless. It must become more than head knowledge. It must become a wisdom of the heart.

Spiritual growth is a process of becoming. It is not past tense. It is always present and future. It continues to evolve. It is an ongoing, fluid, never-ending process in which we continually grow toward wholeness and healing through Christ.

Second, our use of *Christ* instead of *God.* We are in need of salvation, *not* Creation. As Christians, we believe that Christ is our Savior. We also believe that He is our HEALER, because the Greek word for salvation is *heal.*

Therefore, we should use *Christ,* and not *God.* But who is Christ? Yes, He is our Savior and our Healer, but He also comes announcing *life,* not death. He said, "I come that they (we) may have life and have it more abundantly" (John 10:10).

Jesus the Christ came to bless us with a new kind of life, a life of growth and healing. He came to show us the way to obtain GROWTH IN A NEW WAY OF LIVING. We believe that the 12 Steps for Christian Living can help us to accomplish this.

The Christian Way is really very easy to understand, it is just hard to live.

Christ is not only a healer/savior, He also came to show us how to gain wisdom. He *is* our wisdom.

This does not mean that God is not wise. It only means that God's wisdom can better be understood through His example here on earth, Jesus Christ.

In Hebrew scriptures, wisdom which is personified is referred to as a vine "taken root in a privileged people." Jesus also speaks of himself as a vine who is the source of our growth and healing. "I am the vine, you are the branches. Whoever remains (lives) in me and I in him/her, shall produce a large crop of fruit" (John 15:5). The fruits that He refers to are ". . . love, joy, peace, patience, kindness, goodness, faithfulness, gentleness, and self-control. . ." (Galatians 5:22). The healing that Christ wants for us will express itself in these fruits, for He brings wisdom when He shows us that having the right attitude is the key to happiness.

So Christ is the bringer of wisdom here on earth. He shows us that wisdom is found in the simplest of things. Jesus' life is an example of someone who was always searching for wisdom in order to grow in wisdom. Even as a child He was "filled with wisdom" (Luke 2:40) and "increased in wisdom" (Luke 2:52).

Not only did He grow in wisdom, but He personified wisdom. He often was referred to as a royal person (King) who was calling all humankind to their royal personhood. For this He had to pay the ultimate price — death.

The role evolved even though He had no desire to be a king. In fact, He rejects these temptations in Luke 3:21-4:14. He came to redefine kingship and redistribute power equally, so that everyone can realize that he or she has the right to be a king or queen. He paved the way for all of us to be royal persons with dignity and responsibility for the universe.

Even His name Christ, which means "Anointed One" reminds

us that He was given special blessings from God to give to us. In Hebrew, the divinely anointed one is "Messiah." As the Messiah He is to bestow on us God's blessings, so that His people (you and I) might know prosperity, the abundant life.

How do we find the abundant life? He tells us that it is through Him. He is the food. He is all that we need to take with us on our spiritual journey through life. He will give us the nourishment and hope that will result in the abundant life. He says: ". . . the bread of God is that which comes down from heaven and gives life to the world . . . I am the bread of life; he (she) who comes to me shall not hunger . . ." (John 6:33-35).

Thus, Christ will provide for all of the needs we have to find healing and the abundant life. He is our power and our wisdom, and this is all a gift from God through Jesus to us. We only need to receive Christ and we can be healed. He is the way to God's healing and new life.

Christ asks us to follow him so that we might find life. He wants us to come alive. He wants us to trust in him, so that He can empower us and heal us.

He instructs us to follow him through the telling of stories and parables. He shows us a LIFESTYLE for living. This lifestyle promotes the healing of attitudes and the realization that the abundant life is found in the simple values of God's creation.

He also teaches us to pray. He wants us to know that God is a personal God. This is why He calls Him "Abba Father," which means "Papa."

He teaches us how to receive His blessings and pass them on to others. He stated that the greatest blessings are our attitudes, and these are found in the Beatitudes (Matthew 5:3-12). He insists that this new way of thinking is possible for everyone. All that we have to do is be willing to do our part by becoming *entirely ready.*

The third difference in this step is the use of the word *heal* and not *remove.* As I stated earlier in this chapter, I can't believe that God would be so cruel that He would create us one way and then want us to be a different person. I am convinced that He wants our attitudes to be healed but not removed. The reason for this is that some of our character traits have become weaknesses and not strengths. Therefore, they need to be changed.

God created us with certain qualities. However, as we have lived our lives these good qualities have eroded because of the environments in which we have lived. Many of our attitudes have become destructive. They have become, in fact, weaknesses and not strengths.

As a result, we are in need of salvation, we are in need of healing. This is Christ's desire for us. He came to bring about our healing. This is why He gave us the Beatitudes and the rest of the Sermon on the Mount (Matthew 5-7). He wanted to impress upon us the truth that happiness and peace of mind will only be ours if our attitudes are right.

This happiness and peace can be accomplished through the healing of the memories from the past which have resulted in destructive attitudes. If we are willing to allow the love and forgiveness of Christ and His example to show us the way to live, we will experience the spiritual life. Forgiveness is the attitude which promotes the most healing of past memories of hurtful events. When we are willing to forgive the past hurts our attitudes will change, because healing has taken place. Christ's example of forgiveness has given us the power to forgive . . . and we have found a more spiritual lifestyle.

What is a Spiritual Lifestyle?

Living a more spiritual lifestyle, as I see it, involves two aspects: freedom and responsibility.

We need to accept the gift of FREEDOM which Christ brought to us. Through the power of His love and forgiveness He has taught us that we are to be the person God created us to be. Christ was that example. He was faithful to His role at creation. He was God incarnate. He was love in its most perfect human form, even to the point of giving His life for His sisters and brothers.

We too are free. As followers of Christ, we are free. Freed from the burden of having to be perfect, and freed from attempting to achieve perfection by repressing who we are. Christ has shown us that repression only results in bad attitudes and in the desire to hang onto them.

It stifles our desire to love as Christ taught us to love. When we repress our love it ceases to be unconditional and no longer is given freely without any expectations. It becomes selfish, controlling, and manipulative. Christ came to fulfill the law. This means that His emphasis was on what we should do to find the abundant life, not on what we *shouldn't* do.

When we accept the truth which Christ taught, the truth that perfection in Him is a free gift, then we will know what it is to be free.

Yet Jesus did not tell us that He would do it all for us. He reminded us that we have to do our part in the healing process, otherwise we would not experience "a more spiritual lifestyle." Healing and the abundant life require our "work" too. We are to "work out our own salvation (healing) in fear and trembling" (Philippians 2:12).

"Fear" here means respect. We are to trust and follow Christ, who is God incarnate here on earth. He will help us toward that healing process by providing us with courage and direction. BUT WE MUST DO OUR PART!

This is where being responsible comes in. As mature Christians we are to take responsibility for our own growth. It is true that we are not responsible for attaining perfection, but we must do our part if we are to grow spiritually. Our part begins with our readiness for growth.

God wants us to reach our potential for growth. To enable this to happen He has given us the gift of freedom, freedom from having to attain our own perfection. Christ has accomplished this perfection for us in His death and resurrection. In addition, God had Christ show us how to participate in our own growth process. This participation is the part for which we need to be responsible.

Often we want freedom without responsibility, or we want power without accountability. This appears to be nice and easy, but it never works out. It usually results in chaos and abuse. It doesn't bring about a more spiritual lifestyle.

Developing a more spiritual lifestyle requires God's gift of freedom and humankind's delivery of responsibility.

When we change our inner attitudes, we are then able to

change the outer aspects of our lives with Christ's help. Step 7 deals with the transformation of our behavior.

Life Example

Jane had to make a decision about a meaningless marriage. Her dream gave evidence to her that she was entirely ready to change her present attitude which said, "Happiness is how my life looks on the outside." The dream is as follows:

"There was a little girl about five years old standing naked on the top of a high hill that was covered with crusty snow. I know that she was me but I looked like my daughter at the same age. I was looking down the icy landscape feeling scared and vulnerable with my nakedness, knowing that I had to make the trip down the mountain. I didn't see another choice, but felt that, if I didn't die in the process, I would be cut up, bruised, or seriously injured. I felt an enormous wave of sadness, like it was a suicide mission. Looking down, there was a highway below with speeding cars in both lanes. I thought that even if I make it down I would be run over by the oncoming traffic. I felt overwhelmed by the possibility, yet there seemed to be nothing at the top for me — I was alone on the pinnacle. So I plunged headlong down the chasm, like a skier on a long run. I felt only numbness while running, walking and sliding down the steep descent. I gained momentum and lost control, slipping and tumbling head-on. A loud voice penetrated my experience shouting, 'Grab on to the snow fence, grab on to the snow fence!' I woke from the dream feeling both exhausted and relieved, yet unresolved with the experience.

"At that time in my conscious life, I was in the process of leaving a marriage of twenty-five years. It was not a 'bad marriage,' just a relationship that gradually lost meaning. I had often felt isolated and alone — on the pinnacle, so to speak. For years I had applied bandaids to my inner wounds and sought other comfort stations, but only to feel more fragmented and lonely. All the 'right' outer elements were there, but I was not present."

As Jane thought more about her dream, she felt it was God's message to her that He was with her (the snow fence). She was now ready to stop covering up her pain and have Christ heal it.

STEP 6

SCRIPTURES AND AFFIRMATION FOR STEP 6

Life Principle: If nothing changes . . . nothing changes.

Read, meditate, and journal on the following Scripture passages. There is one for each day of the week. Then use the corresponding affirmation as a daily reminder that Christ can heal my destructive attitudes so that I can experience both freedom and responsibility.

John 5:5 — With Jesus I can do all things.
Psalms 41:4 — When I'm honest I can be healed.
Philippians 2:12 — I'll do my part.
John 6:33-35 — Jesus is all I need.
Ephesians 4:22-24 — The healing of memories is the key to new attitudes.
Psalm 34:4 — I am freed of fear.
Galatians 5:22-23 — I am filled with the fruits of the Spirit.

PRAYER

Forgive me for the sin of unwillingness, and fill me with the spirit of your gifts.

Amen.

STEP SEVEN

"We humbly ask Christ to transform all of our shortcomings!"[1]

Change is Constant

A change in the way we think is our starting point when we allow Christ to transform our lives. And when He heals our destructive attitudes, that healing can result in a change in behavior as well. Yet, it is one thing to have Christ heal our character defects, and it is another thing to have Christ transform our behavior.

Perhaps 90% of becoming that new person in Christ (Colossians 3:10) involves a change in the behavior that hurts and separates us from others and God. This is only possible with Christ's help and our willingness to do our part.

God has provided us with the talents at creation to fill life with meaning and also to make a worthwhile contribution to the world. What we do with these gifts is entirely up to us. We can minimize them and thereby not use them to reach our potential for growth, or we can embrace them and nurture them, so that we accentuate our strengths and are open to changing our weaknesses. We can choose an empty life, or we can pursue life to its fullest.

If we wish to use our giftedness, we need to desire growth and change. We need to both heal the way we think and transform the way we act.

[1]V. Bittner, *Breaking Free*, p. 123 - Revised from the original writing in *You Can Help With Your Healing*, p. 144.

Unless we admit to our need for change, we will probably be changing in ways that lead to a more destructive lifestyle. Change is constant. What is important is that we accept this truth and work with it, rather than let it happen without our knowing it. If we work with it, we will be able to change more positively.

This is why we use the present tense of the verb "to ask." Change is a part of life, it is ongoing. Therefore, we must accept the truths that change is constant and also that growth toward wholeness and happiness is both present and future. Transforming our behavior is a never-ending process in which we participate, so that we might be the person that God created us to be.

To Trust is to be Transformed

Becoming humble means facing the reality that positive change is possible when we *trust* Christ's power to help us in our transformation. The kind of trust that is necessary for the power of Christ to transform behavior is three-fold.

First, it is *self-trust.* One of the most defeating kinds of behavior is not believing in ourselves. I can remember the man who had everything going for him. He had a beautiful wife and child and an excellent job. Then, through circumstances beyond his control, his business fell apart. As a result, he was so shattered that his marriage began to fail as well.

One day I saw him alone, and the message that I heard from him was that he had given up. He said, "Why should I try to help myself by changing my behavior? It won't do any good anyway. I have already lost my business, and now my wife wants to leave me."

He had no self-trust. Many of us have experienced this feeling. If we have gone through some hard times we have probably experienced some hopelessness. At such times we need to call upon all of our resources to do what is necessary to help ourselves, even if we don't feel like doing it.

If we don't like what we do, we can't like ourselves . . . and if we continue to avoid changing our destructive behavior, we will feel even worse. Then we are in a downward spiral, and the negative feelings about ourselves multiply.

The only way we can correct this destructive cycle is to ACT, even though we don't feel like acting.

Feeling better about ourselves doesn't just happen. Perhaps some of us wished that Christ would transform our shortcomings for us, or that God would just "zap" us so we could have self-trust. Unfortunately, it doesn't work that way most of the time . . . and waiting to feel better often becomes an excuse to remain miserable, helpless, and hopeless. Self-trust comes primarily through new behavior. The more we like ourselves (self-trust) for what we do, the more we are able to have Christ help us transform our life.

The second kind of trust that is necessary for transformation is *other-trust.* Change is not possible alone. We need the help of others.

One of the statements we make to those who are interested in starting a 12 Steps for Christian Living group is: "Growth is best accomplished by sharing our spiritual journey with others and having them share theirs with us." In our spiritual journey we include both our strengths and weaknesses, as well as our victories and failures. To share these experiences, plus the way we grew or why we failed can be one of the most powerful gifts we can receive from one another.

This is why the Christian community is so valuable. When we refuse to accept this truth, we are rejecting God and His purpose at creation. He created us for relationships. This is why He not only created man AND woman, but all the rest of creation as well.

The third aspect of trust is *God-trust.* We need to believe that the power of God's presence in Christ is within us and around us and will empower us to do what is necessary to be transformed.

Many times when we are going through the desert experiences of our life, we have difficulty trusting the fact that Christ is present with us. We seem to feel that we are all alone in this struggle for new behavior.

Yet, often we are reminded that it is the experience of living through both joy and sorrow which most convinces us that God is still in charge. In Romans 5:3-5 Paul says:

"We can rejoice, too, when we run into problems and trials for we know that they are good for us — they help us learn to be patient. And patience develops strength of character in us and helps us trust God more each time we use it until finally our hope and faith (trust) are strong and steady. Then, when that happens, we are able to hold our heads high no matter what happens and know that all is well, for we know how dearly God loves us, and we feel this warm love everywhere within us because God has given us the Holy Spirit to fill our hearts with His love."

Here Paul is telling us that the best way that we can possibly know God's love is to experience His presence through the trials of life. Therefore, we know God's love most of all by living the process. Then we will have evidence that God is still in charge. We will also experience the empowering presence of Christ to help us change what we can change and accept what we cannot change.

God-trust comes with living life as it is — both the light and dark side as well as the joy and pain. Trust is the result of experiencing all of life, and this includes our relationship to self, others and God.

Perhaps what God empowers us the most to trust, however, is that God sees us not as we are, rather He sees our potential. This is why He sent His son to die for us. Through the sacrifice of His son, He makes it possible for us to be transformed with Christ's help through the power of His forgiveness. By forgiving us He sees what we potentially could be. Through transformation God empowers us to grow, to become the people we can be.

I believe that nothing promotes trust more than believing in another person's potential. When we know that God is treating us as if we had already become what we potentially could be, He empowers us to be what we are to be. This is unconditional love! It is this kind of behavior on the part of God that builds our trust — trust not only in Him, but in others and ourselves as well.

Christ's example has given us this ability to trust God. Without this kind of trust, growth and transformation would be impossible. We would not be able to achieve it through our own power. Change will take place only when we humbly admit that we need this gift of trust, this gift of God's unconditional love.

No Transformation without Death

Transformation is not the work of God, but the result of the labor of Christ. In Step 7 we have changed the wording from "God" to "Christ." God is the creator and Christ is the redeemer. Through the faithfulness of Jesus we have been delivered from the consequences of sin — death. He died for us so that we might experience resurrection and transformation — new life.

When we look at nature, we learn that all things have a cycle of life, death, and transformation. In Minnesota the brilliant autumn colors of gold and red remind us that the leaves are saying goodbye. Their beauty is perhaps their way of saying thank you for life. Yet, they are being prepared to vacate this life for another. They will become food for another generation of leaves.

The cycle of nature offers no evidence that death is to be feared, nor does it offer any thought that there is fear in new life or new beginnings. Even death can be trusted, even transformation. In fact, we can see by this process of nature that death, too, has value.

Our growth usually starts with new thoughts which begin to germinate into new behavior. The new way of thinking may be as tiny as a "mustard seed," but it can grow into a beautiful flower. As our life progresses we continue to be transformed by our many deaths into new life of many kinds.

However, this life (or our lifestyle) can be positive or negative. When our destructive attitudes are being healed (Step 6) we are in a better position to let our negative behavior die. Yet, this death does not come automatically.

To illustrate, I think of my own experience. My mother died when I was seven years old. At age thirty-five I became aware that I had not resolved the grief of this loss. I immediately made the decision to let go of this pain so I could get on with my life. Up to that time, I had not married. Unconsciously, I had been afraid of losing again, so I chose not to get too close to anyone. It wasn't until age fifty-three that I made the choice to get married.

This illustrates that new or different behavior does not follow immediately after the healing of memories. Transformation of our behavior takes time, and it is an evolving process. There had to be a lot of dying in my life in order for me to reach the point of marriage.

Transformation is dying to old destructive behavior and coming alive to a new, more positive lifestyle in Christ.

Transformation is New Behavior

The dictionary definition of transformation is: "To change in outward form, shape or semblance."[1] In other words, to be transformed by Christ means that our behavior is in the process of changing from shortcomings to a more adequate lifestyle.

In II Corinthians 5:17, Paul tells us that when we have become Christian, we are "not the same anymore." We are transformed and we are a new creation.

In the other 12 step programs, there is an obvious exclusion of the word "sin(s)." In Steps 1 and 5, we use this word. The words the other 12 step programs use are "unmanageable" and "wrongs." They imply that these destructive attitudes and behaviors are *only* a disease. I find this hard to believe. I am convinced that negative attitudes and behaviors are both a sign of illness and of SIN.

There is no doubt that destructive living is a disease. As the "Big Book" of *Alcoholics Anonymous* says:

> *"It helped me a great deal to become convinced that alcoholism was a disease, not a moral issue; that I had been drinking as a result of compulsion, even though I had not been aware of the compulsion at the time; and that sobriety was not a matter of willpower."*[2]

[1] *Webster's New Collegiate Dictionary*, 1945, p. 903.
[2] *Alcoholics Anonymous*, New and Revised Edition, Alcoholics Anonymous World Service, Inc., New York City, 1955.

If this is true, then all immature behavior is a disease . . . and one could conclude that it is. We are all sick in some sense.

Then the logic that follows this kind of reasoning is that I have not caused destructive attitudes and behaviors. I cannot cure them and I cannot control them. *But I am responsible for my behavior with regard to them.*

I don't completely understand this line of reasoning. Nor do I understand that, first of all, in order to work on my "spirituality" I have to do away with sin. The denial of sin may be, in fact, the inability to accept Step 1. It may also be just a form of mental gymnastics so that one can reach the point of moving beyond guilt to be able to work on the disease as well as the sin. Besides, if it isn't sin, why then do I need to work on making amends in Steps 8 and 9?

I realize that working on our spirituality has to be seen as spiritual growth, rather than spiritual perfection. However, just because we cannot obtain perfection does not mean that we have to do away with "sin." Sin still exists. It is still a part of the way we live, whether we are sick or not. And, certainly, the result of our destructive behavior is sin.

If we are responsible for our behavior that results from our disease, why do we have so much difficulty calling it sin? This would seem to be the most logical name to use. Sin is anything that separates us from God, others, or ourselves.

We can choose to call irresponsible behavior whatever we wish, but I believe it is both disease *and* sin. To see the 12 Steps as presented in the 12 Steps for Christian Living helps us to avoid denial and to name destructive behavior for what it really is — sin. When we do this we have a better chance to grow spiritually because we are being honest. When we face reality the 12 Steps will work for us. Yet, it is hard to know why they do, except for the fact that the 12 Steps for Christian Living contain the basic concepts of the Christian faith. When they are followed as a structure for life, they become a lifestyle. A "faith" system can only become significant if it becomes a way of life.

As we have written the 12 Steps, they are an expression of the Christian faith put into practice. Our program has only existed for eight years, but it has worked miracles of healing and transformation in the lives of those who have worked the steps.

It is interesting that the medical model has not been able to help with those who express destructive emotional and spiritual behavior. The reason for this is their primary focus on the body and their tendency to ignore the emotional and spiritual side of humankind. But medical physicians are now beginning to see that they cannot treat even the physical problems by just concentrating on the body. They are beginning to see human beings in a wholistic sense, as people who are psychospiritual as well.

Destructive, sinful behavior is essentially a spiritual breakdown. It is a journey away from that which brings about happiness. It is a journey into spiritual and emotional blindness and apathy. When we seek after the superficial values of life we are into delusion, denial, and separation. We need to grow in a new way of living through the transforming power of Jesus Christ.

How then do we move from destructive behavior to spiritual growth and transformation? We do this by asking Christ daily to transform our lives and by being willing to do our part.

Life Example

The following dream occurred after Jean had attempted some marriage counseling. She still felt a need to separate herself from the marriage, but had not yet done so. It was summer, and she and her husband and son were at a picnic area. They went to park the car while she explored the surrounding area. She moved to the edge of a cliff and saw some rushing water below. All of a sudden the ground gave way and she started slipping, but she held on to the ground and yelled for help. Her husband and son were busy watching some cheerleaders practice and didn't notice her dilemma. She remembered, "I had to help myself, but I was afraid that I would lose my contact lenses and, worse yet, would be swept away and drowned in the rushing water." She couldn't hold on any longer. She was tired and the ground was eroding beneath her. Her inner voice said softly, "Just take it easy and you'll be all right." She listened this time. She slowly went down the cliff on her stomach, feet first. The damp soil was crumbling, full of rocks and difficult to hang on to. She reached the bottom fairly easily, but her neat image was destroyed in the descent. She laughed at herself! She found that the water, though moving fast, was not that deep and the crossing was not that wide. So she waded into the cold, knee-deep water, stepping on the slippery rocks until she got across to the other side. A short distance away there was a set of steps hewn out of rock that looked as if it had been climbed before by many people. She climbed to the top with little difficulty. Then she awakened. She later had the feeling that she had moved significantly in her growth but still felt unfinished, as she didn't know what would happen now that she was on the other side.

From the dream, it seems apparent that Jean wanted to change her exterior behavior. She was tired of the facade. The dream also points out that transformation is an ongoing process. Now that she had changed some of her destructive behavior she still had to deal with the form her new lifestyle would take and the direction she was going with her life.

STEP 7

SCRIPTURES AND AFFIRMATION FOR STEP 7

Life Principle: I'm becoming brand new!

Read, meditate, and journal on the following Scripture passages. There is one for each day of the week. Then use the corresponding affirmation as a daily reminder that Christ's transformation of our destructive behavior is possible when we trust ourselves, others and God.

Romans 5:1-2	— Humility is becoming all I can become.
Matthew 7:7-8	— If I ask, I will receive.
Colossians 3:10	— I am becoming more like Christ.
Romans 5:3-5	— I believe therefore I can become.
Romans 12:1-2	— Transformation is the key to serenity.
Galatians 6:15	— Being transformed is what counts.
II Corinthians 5:17	— I'm a Christian and I'm becoming brand new.

PRAYER

Jesus, I admit that changing my destructive behavior is impossible without your help. Thank you for making it happen!

Amen.

STEP EIGHT

"We make a list of all persons we have harmed and become willing to make amends to them all."[1]

We Need to Shed our Mask

In Step 4, with the Institute for Christian Living's 4th Step Inventory, we have the opportunity to look at more than our past sins. There is the encouragement to also look at our history in order that we might discover why we are the way we are. In addition, there is the opportunity to perhaps get in touch with some of the individuals in our lives to whom we need to make amends.

The recommendation of step 8 is that we *write* their names. This is the only step in which we are told to do any writing. Those of us who want to grow spiritually and emotionally know its value. Writing helps us to see what is going on inside.

Often we discover our subconscious through writing. This is perhaps the best way to shed our outer mask. The mask is the person we pretend to be. It is the person we show the world, but it is a contradiction. The mask hides our real feelings, needs, and values. Many of us have pretended for so long that we have even fooled ourselves regarding who we truly are.

The mask has some values because without it some of us would not have any defenses. We need some protection at times to

[1]V. Bittner, *You Can Help With Your Healing*, p. 144.

get along in a hostile world. Yet, the mask has a tendency to be more destructive than constructive, because we come to believe we are the person we pretend to be.

Playing a role can get very tiresome. But the most destructive effect is the destruction of our creativity. This happens because there is a conflict between our inner and outer life. To keep this contradiction going takes a lot of energy, so much in fact, that we don't have any left to be creative.

The false front needs to go. Working step 8 can help us get rid of it. As we write down the names of those persons with whom we need to make amends, we help shed the mask. We get in contact with the people and events in our past that need reconciliation.

This tendency to wear a mask is not unique to us. Jesus speaks of this often in regard to the Pharisees. He calls them hypocrites. He is more concerned about this sin because it is a sin of the spirit and not a sin of the flesh.

The Pharisees were virtuous people when it came to the sins of the flesh. Their major failings were with the sin of the spirit, for they were pretending to be something other than what they were. The sin of the spirit can destroy the soul. Jesus knew this, and that is why He said: "...if your virtue goes no deeper than that of the scribes and Pharisees, you will never get into the Kingdom of heaven" (Matthew 5:20).

Jesus said this because He knew there were two sides to all of us – an inner and outer self. Only the ethic which reaches to the deepest part (the heart) of a person is fit for the kingdom or the abundant life.

The persons who take their "heart" (unconscious) seriously are the ones who will be able to accept that part of themselves and thereby be able to work on reconciling the inner with the outer. When we do this, we discover authenticity and also serenity because we are not trying to project something other than what we are! Step 8 can help us to accomplish this.

Our greatest delusion is thinking that we can avoid the subconscious and solve the moral issues of life by creating a righteous exterior. We need to face the person within and see if we are holding on to any guilt or resentment toward any of the important people in our lives. We need to visually encounter the names of the people with whom we need to make amends. Some of us may have several names. Some may find that making amends is primarily with themselves, and others may have difficulty coming up with any names at all. This is not that uncommon, especially if we have been people pleasers. Yet, doing things to please others may not always be the most kind thing to do. In the long run, pleasing others may be more hurtful than not doing what they ask. It could only be encouraging them to be irresponsible and dependent on us.

If this is true, we may find that we will have some names on our list after all. Certainly, we will know that always pleasing others has many times hurt us, if not them.

Honesty is Painful

When I think of making amends, I think of it in two ways: making a list of those I have hurt, and making a list of those who have hurt me. In other words, it means being willing to apologize to those I have hurt, as well as forgive those who have hurt me.

The process of getting in touch with these individuals in our past can be very painful. This is why steps 8 and 9 are so difficult. Not only do they involve digging up our subconscious, but also acting out new behavior – making direct amends (Step 9).

One of the most important steps in "Growth in a New Way of Living," the 4th Step Inventory Worksheet (Appendix 1), is *looking* at the way our past history really was and *sharing* it. Steps 8 and 9 help us to face the pain.

If only we could learn that there is much to be gained through pain. Pain is so frightening for most of us. We are willing to do almost anything to avoid it. We become TV addicts, workaholics, foodaholics, or alcoholics. We are a people who run from solitude because we might incur some pain. We are a culture that has not learned to deal with pain. So we deny its existence.

Making a list is facing pain head on. In the 12 Steps for Christian Living we again use the present tense of the verb "make." We want to emphasize that this step and the other ones are not done only once. They are done over and over again. They must become a part of our lifestyle.

Being conscious of the persons with whom we need to make amends is a daily process. It is something for the present and the future. The more we do it, the easier it will become.

Encountering the repressed pain that we have induced or incurred in our life is an important part of the healing process. In order to resolve it, though, we need to enter into it by making a list.

Continuing to cover up our guilt for not apologizing and our resentment for not forgiving is in reality, a decision to keep the pain. As a consequence we have to cover the pain with something and this does not release it. Instead, pain runs our life. We are out of control.

When we admit the pain, by allowing it to emerge, we need courage. Perhaps courage is the most essential virtue on our spiritual journey. And this is why it is so comforting to know that Jesus is on the journey with us.

Allow Pain to be Pain

If we fail to let pain be pain, it will haunt us in destructive ways. It will prevent us from being the creative healers God has called us to be. Instead, we will be the victims of pain and then often the victimizers of others.

For these reasons making amends is so vital to our spiritual growth. Unless we deal with our pain by making amends, we will either continue to hurt others because of our unresolved pain, or we will live out the premise that we deserve pain and continue to put ourselves in abusive situations. Unless we befriend our pain, unless we embrace the people we have harmed by *writing* a list, we will not be able to let go. There is no way of letting go of the pain induced or incurred in life without naming it. This gives us power to let go.

Step 8 incorporates, then, three parts. First, making amends involves embracing this pain in our lives and allowing those painful experiences to emerge from the subconscious. Next, we need to be with that pain for a while. Writing down the names of those harmed can help us to do that. Finally, after we have lived with the pain for a while, we are ready to do what we need to do to let go of it.

This is the process involved in working Step 8. When we act on the three parts mentioned above we hopefully will be "willing to make amends to them all." We will want to get rid of the pain.

Many people are not willing to make amends because they have continued to live in denial of their pain. However, there is energy in pain!

How Does Pain Enliven Us?

First, our pain can help us to be understanding of the pain of others. If we have hurt another person it might be difficult to be motivated to reach out to that person unless we understand what it is like to be in pain – especially the pain of being estranged.

Pain is not a private affair. It is a social experience. So, too, is making amends. This presupposes a relationship, most likely a broken one.

When we allow ourselves to let pain be pain, we learn compassion. I am not sure that there is any other way to learn it. When we have suffered pain by embracing it and allowing it to exist in our lives, we can easily see it in others. Pain is perhaps the most legitimate way that we grow in our ability to identify with others.

Pain teaches us compassion! Pain helps us to be understanding of others, in other words, to be compassionate.

The *second* way pain helps us to become entirely ready to make amends is by helping us to discern what truly makes life beautiful.

Not only do we understand what can bring us the abundant life, but we realize that much of the way we have lived has only brought us pain. By dealing with the pain of encountering those with whom we need to make amends, we realize that what makes life beautiful is not the "fixes" in life. It is the relationships with the important people in our life.

When we are wearing our masks and hiding the inner self, we tend to lose touch with what it is that makes life precious. When we don't allow pain to emerge, we spend all of our energy trying to keep it covered. In the process, we lose our love for life, because we are exhausted from our attempts to keep everything pushed down.

The process of becoming ready to make amends will help us bring back a love for life. We will discover the key to help us find the abundant life. That key is reconciliation, through the making of amends.

The *third* energizing aspect of pain is its ability to strengthen us. As we get in touch with those individuals whom we have hurt or who have hurt us, we grow stronger. The more we avoid pain, the more fearful of it we become.

The opposite is also true. The more we face the painful experiences of our misconduct and our unforgiveness, the easier it will be to face pain in the future.

This is spiritual growth! Growth is a process. If we avoid dealing with certain people in our lives, they will continue to haunt us and will prevent us from being the creative wounded healers we can become.

Paul says that we can rejoice when we endure suffering, because this teaches us patience, and patience helps us to become strong within ourselves and strong in our trust of God (Romans 5:3-5).

So pain not only strengthens our own self-reliance, but our reliance on God!

The *fourth* way pain can enliven us is to help us share our pain. A part of making amends is to tell others about our pain. It is one thing to apologize for the wrong we have done to others, and it is another thing to tell them how we feel they have wronged us.

Often this is the most crucial aspect in the process of making amends. If we do not deal with our own pain of feeling abused we will be immobilized. This pain will lead to resentment, and the resentment will cause us to sink into apathy. We will then be without any energy or motivation to make amends. In fact, we will be prone to let it go by doing nothing.

Apathy is a form of death. It is dying inside, and this is the worst death of all.

Letting our pain surface can help us to use the pain of guilt and of unforgiveness, enlivening us to share it. This is making direct amends.[1]

Fifth, pain enlivens us by opening us up to others, God, and the universe. A part of making amends is admitting our oneness in sin, guilt, and unforgiveness.

Paul tells us to bear one another's burdens, and when we do this we are doing what Christ told us to do through His example of suffering for us and with us on the cross (Galatians 6:2).

Everyone suffers. Everyone is in pain. The need for making amends is a part of everyone's life. We all sin and, because of sin, we not only cause pain, but we endure pain. Therefore, we are all in need of making amends.

The pain of allowing pain to be pain helps us to become willing to make amends. This is the process that energizes us to be willing. This is the process, too, that prepares us for step 9 — to "make direct amends . . . except when to do so would injure them or others."[2]

Finally, the pain which results from the need for making amends should not be glorified. This is important. To let pain be pain does not mean that we wallow in it. Then pain becomes our master.

The purpose of letting pain be pain is to *let go of it.* We do this by making amends. The way that we make amends is by making a list and specifically naming the people with whom we need to be reconciled. Then we need to live with the pain surrounding the people we have named so that, motivated by the pain, we can in Step 9 be ready to make direct amends.

Life Example

John was struggling with making amends. He knew that he had some unfinished business with his father. As a child he had been the recipient of a great deal of abuse, both physical and verbal. I had asked him to journal about these experiences with his father so that he could get in touch with the pain. I had hoped that this would motivate him to move to resolve the guilt he felt as a

[1,2]V. Bittner, *You Can Help With Your Healing,* (Step 9), p. 144.

result of his anger at his father and also to let go of his unforgiveness. That night he had the following dream:

In his dream he was in a rented room. No one thought that this hole in the cellar could have been made livable. However, he had made the room beautiful and comfortable. He was very proud of it and felt good about it. It was someplace that he could call his own. Suddenly, he heard a voice that told him he had to leave the room.

As we talked about the dream he realized that the cellar was his subconscious which was being straightened out because he was getting in touch with it. The fact that he was going to have to leave the cellar was saying that he had lived with the pain long enough. It also said that he deserved more than a basement room. Rather, he should have a room filled with light, color, and beauty. He was ready now to deal with the pain surrounding his father and get on with life. *He was willing to make amends so he could enjoy life.*

STEP 8

SCRIPTURES AND AFFIRMATION FOR STEP 8

Life Principle: Let pain be pain . . . and grow through it.

Read, meditate and journal on the following Scripture passages. There is one for each day of the week. Then use the corresponding affirmation as a daily reminder that being willing to make amends is motivated by allowing our pain of guilt and unforgiveness to emerge.

Philippians 2:3-4	—	Happiness is found in being humble.
Matthew 6:4	—	God sees us and loves us as we are.
Matthew 5:20	—	Honesty is the key to happiness.
Matthew 5:44	—	I will love my enemies.
I John 4:20-21	—	To love God means I also love my neighbor.
Matthew 22:37-39	—	I will love God, others and myself.
Galatians 6:2	—	I am not alone in my suffering.

PRAYER

Help me to name those with whom I need to be reconciled so that I will be energized to make amends.

Amen.

STEP NINE

"We make direct amends to such persons wherever possible, except when to do so would injure them or others."[1]

To Make Amends is to Learn Compassion

For us to only be a vessel or a recipient of love and compassion is not enough. we must be a channel of God's love. Now that we have become willing to make amends, we must act on that decision. Step 9 gives us the chance to finally make up for past wrongs, even though we can never fully do this. It is the opportunity to lighten the weight we have been carrying for so long. Hopefully, as this step indicates, it will make other people feel better. Yet, when we make amends, we will ultimately feel better than anyone else.

In *Webster's New Collegiate Dictionary*, we are told that compassion is "pity." This is a pathetic definition, because pity denotes a superior/inferior relationship. Obviously, compassion that is expressed by equals seems to be obsolete.

The reduction of compassion to sentimental, philanthropic relationships tells us much about the degeneration of our culture. In addition, it leaves us ignorant about what compassion really is.

Jesus tells us that we are to be "compassionate as God is compassionate (Luke 6:36).

Real compassion requires equality, not a superior/inferior re-

[1]V. Bittner, *You Can Help With Your Healing*, p. 144.

lationship. Making amends for the guilt and unforgiveness that we have carried around needs to be done not because we feel either better or worse than those to whom we go, but because we know we are EQUAL. This motivation involves not only understanding compassion, but practicing it as well.

What we are talking about here is a relationship of interdependence. Often when we use this step, we could have the fantasy that we must be in a position of humiliation. This is not equality.

Some often have the misconstrued idea that, because of their guilt or unforgiveness, they must be disgraced if they are to correctly do the 9th step. Their misconception is that unless they feel shame they cannot expect forgiveness. Being penitent does not mean we must be degraded for our sins.

God didn't ask us to wallow. He only asked that we desire to change our life. Here is the true meaning of being penitent. We have to want to change our life around. In fact, the way we express this desire is by going directly to those we have wronged and admit our sin in person.

This is not a degrading act. It is, rather, a HUMANE act. We are admitting that we are human, too, just as they are human. We are equal to them, not beneath them.

How to Learn Compassion

The only way to understand compassion is to enter into the process. We must do it. We need to make direct amends; otherwise we won't learn compassion.

We can only understand another's pain when we enter into it. In the same way, we can only know someone's joy when we participate in it. This, then, is being compassionate. We have compassion when we *enter into the life of others in such a way that we experience both their joys and sorrows with them.*

What happens to another happens to us. Even Jesus said, "Whenever you do it to one of these little ones, you do it to me" (Matthew 25:40). This is interdependence. Therefore, when we do what we can to make direct amends we are not only learning compassion, but we are teaching others compassion.

One, however, does not automatically follow the other. Just

because we want to show compassion by making amends, we have no guarantee that others will receive us with understanding, or even desire to learn compassion from us.

We Must be Compassionate to Ourselves

In order to make direct amends to those we have hurt or those who have hurt us, we have to let go of our ego. By this, I am not suggesting that we are to reject ourselves. Rather, we must abandon a view of ourselves as unique; we are just like everyone else, in the sense that we are all sinners.

Here I am not talking about cutting ourselves off from who we are — that is our individuality. Rather, I am asking that we befriend the deeper self within. When we do this we realize that in the depths of our being we are all very much alike. We all have similar needs and feelings. They are just expressed in different ways.

Jesus says that we are to "love others as we love ourselves" (Matthew 22:39). We need to love ourselves compassionately. We need to make amends with ourselves. However, sometimes it is hard to do this unless we first forgive the important others in our life. When we forgive, we will feel that we are more deserving of compassion and forgiveness.

We need to befriend the depths of our being, which is what we work on in Step 4. However, we also work on it in Step 8. Here we allow pain to be pain. We face the people and issues we need to resolve by writing them down. Then, in Step 9 we act on the energy we experience from uncovering our pain of guilt and unforgiveness. Therefore, making amends is learning compassion only if we live it out. The way this is done is by making *direct* amends.

The Value of Making Direct Amends

Learning the value of making direct amends is difficult in our culture. Making amends demands that we become aware of our feelings, rather than our thoughts. Our economic system divorces us from feeling, because it defines the good life in terms of profit rather than human need.

Human need involves our feelings. Reconciliation with those we have hurt or who have hurt us involves our feelings. It involves our worth, our interconnectedness, our pain, and the power we can experience through the reconciliation of making direct amends, which then enables us to be instruments of change and transformation.

As humans we have the innate desire to join with one another. We desire to reach out, to value, to get in touch with the concrete feelings of people, rather than to live in the abstract. Life cannot be lived creatively and meaningfully in a second-handed way.

Making direct amends involves us with the personal, not the impersonal. In this process healing happens, the healing of feelings and attitudes. When this encounter takes place between us and the person with whom we wish to be reconciled, we experience empowerment. Through the process of making direct amends we become prepared to be channels for God's love and healing.

If we miss this connection which becomes possible through making direct amends, we miss life and the fact that it is to be celebrated. To leave out the healing of our feelings is to rob ourselves of the abundant life.

Even God is not an unmoved mover. He was so moved by our condition that He sent His Son to die for us. God is a true participant in life. I not only believe that He danced the day we were born, but He is tickled with joy by the way we sometimes act.

If we are created in His image, then we, too, are created to be involved. We, too, are destined to celebrate life and chosen to experience the abundant life.

This will happen when we accept our humanness, and stop denying our need for the healing of feelings.

When we take seriously our need to make direct amends, we not only will be able to celebrate life, but we will be able to celebrate death. WE WILL BE ABLE TO PLAY!

Ashley Montagu tells us that only the human is capable of continuing to play into adulthood. A fly never plays and even a monkey stops playing when it becomes adult. But we humans can play right up to our death . . . and even with death. As humans, we can even celebrate death.

But how human are we? Unless we accept our need for the

healing of feelings, we will rob ourselves of the right to play, even into adulthood. We will cheat ourselves of the gift of coming alive. We will deprive ourselves of the abundant life.

Only when we come together with those with whom we need to make amends will we be able to celebrate life. When people come together and meet eye to eye, feelings are shared and healed. When we have the courage to go in person to those we have harmed, we are willing to be vulnerable enough to be healed. This is the value of making direct amends.

Making Amends is to Learn Justice

Perhaps the most basic kind of false dependencies and independencies are those involving injustice. The relationships that are either abusive or nonexistent tend to be unjust. The only way to undo the injustice of destructive relationships is to make amends. When we are willing to reach out to those who have been mistreated, healing can take place.

To right an injustice there needs to be a *claim* of injustice and a willingness to be *responsible* for setting things right. When we are making direct amends we respond to the claim of injustice.

Making direct amends is not a win/lose situation. Perhaps some feel that the one who reaches out to make direct amends is the loser. However, this is not true. For if we can help in the healing of an injustice, we have helped ourselves. When our loved ones are in pain, we are in pain as well. To relieve another's pain by taking our part of the responsibility is to relieve our own pain and also the pain of God, who shares in everyone's hurt.

Those who advocate that we should not be co-dependent would probably be upset by the paragraph above. It is true that if almost all of our good feelings would come from the good feelings of others, we would have a problem. Yet, I believe that some co-dependency is necessary, otherwise we wouldn't need anyone. In addition, we probably wouldn't care what happened to other people. We especially would have no need to be the "Good Samaritan." In the Bible apathy, not hate, is the opposite of love.

Therefore, making direct amends is only a WIN situation, whether there is a reconciliation or not. If we are willing to right an injustice, we have learned justice. What the other people do with the amends attempt is up to them. They can reject our attempt or accept it. Either way we win because we are learning justice, and we have done our part.

Finally, if we are really learning justice, we will seek out and find the one to whom we need to make amends. Only those who are honestly committed to justice are willing to seek out those who have been treated unjustly.

When we are sincerely intent about making direct amends, we cannot wait comfortably for the persons to come knocking on our door. We need to seek them out, just as a lover seeks out his/her beloved.

To make direct amends is to learn justice and to communicate the same to those we seek out.

Making Amends with Oneself

Undoubtedly, the person we have the most difficulty apologizing to and forgiving is ourselves. Jesus calls all of us to reconciliation with one another, God, *and* ourselves.

Jesus taught us to love ourselves, forgive ourselves, and recognize the spark of divine within us. This is where learning to love God begins. Because we have been loved, we can love. We can make amends. We can only experience God's love through self-acceptance.

Therefore, unless we make direct amends with ourselves, we will have difficulty making direct amends to others. The opposite is true. It will be hard for us to love ourselves if we have not made direct amends with the important people in our lives.

Jesus wanted us to be compassionate toward ourselves. He told us to love others as we love ourselves. In fact, He was so concerned about our making amends with ourselves that He died on a cross. In doing this He freed us from self-hatred and masochism. He freed us to feel compassion for ourselves. Finally, He freed us from pessimism, which is the basis for sadism.

Self-hatred is the cause of our unwillingness to make amends, whether direct or indirect. When we hate ourselves we will hate the world. We can even justify keeping our resentment by pretending that others and the world are bad, so they can be the object of our hatred instead of ourselves.

Making direct amends with ourselves may be the most difficult part of Step 9. But it is the key to resolving guilt and unforgiveness.

When is Making Amends Destructive?

Becoming ready to apologize and forgive is a two-fold process. Step 8 is getting prepared. In Step 8 we choose to do it, and in Step 9 we carry it out.

Both apologizing and forgiving are two-fold processes, as well. First, we need to choose to let go of guilt (usually due to an unwillingness to apologize) and unforgiveness. Second, we need to accept the fact that such release is a process. When we apologize we are actively making amends to others and ourselves. When we forgive, we are carrying out a process.

Forgiveness usually doesn't happen overnight. We not only need to tell people that we forgive them at times, but we need to overtly say to ourselves, "I will forgive those with whom I am angry." It must become a way of life. In fact, being both apologetic and forgiving need to become intuitive, to become a lifestyle.

The key to acting on the feelings of guilt and forgiveness is our desire not to injure others. Sometimes, not making direct amends could be an avoidance tactic. We tell ourselves we don't want to make amends to someone because we will injure them, when in reality we are afraid they might be angry at us or hurt us.

In other words, sometimes we don't make amends because *we* are afraid of being hurt. It is true that making amends may hurt both parties involved. At times, that can be expected. But there is a difference between hurt and injury.

Injury implies an *intention* to harm someone, whereas hurt does not. We cannot live with people we love without inadvertently hurting them. Hurt often is an unintentional act, but injury is a purposeful act.

If we are out to harm someone, we have entered into the act of making amends for the wrong reason. Our attitude is all-important. When we are making direct amends out of love for others and ourselves we will not injure others or ourselves. But if we are still feeling vindictive, or are trying to atone for our own sin because we do not accept the truth that Jesus has already done this for us, we could be inflicting injury.

What we have prepared for and carried out in Step 8 and 9 have hopefully prepared us for Step 10. Step 10 is a continuation of these two steps on a daily basis.

Life Example

Kim was working through some feelings of the past that had plagued him most of his life. They were associated with his father. He had felt abused by his father as a child. Kim also expressed lack of control at times by "losing it" with his own boys. This bothered him a great deal, because he realized that he was doing to his sons what his father had done to him.

I told him that he was going to have to go to his father and tell him that he wanted to forgive him. This was a difficult decision for Kim. His first thought was that his father might not understand what he was talking about. Yet, he had had some indication that his father wanted to make amends too, but didn't know how.

After the session, he recorded a dream that he had. In the dream he was a teenager. He was riding up a steep hill on his motorcycle. Having been told to be careful, he could feel that he was angry at his father. He had just left his father. All at once the motorcycle stalled and began sliding backwards down toward a very deep lake. Kim was filled with fear.

Suddenly, he felt a hand pulling him toward shore and out of the deep water. When he got to shore, he discovered that the hand was his father's.

As he awoke, he remembered having mixed feelings, both joy and reserve. Perhaps dreaming about his father being there for him was what Kim had desired, but up to now had not experienced. He wanted that closeness. At least he was willing to see if it could possibly happen.

That same morning he called his father. They got together and talked about their relationship. At this time I am not aware of what happened as a result of this meeting. Most importantly, the dream helped Kim find the courage to make direct amends with his father by dealing with his unforgiveness.

Kim discovered that the dream was a way in which his inner life spoke to him. Often the message which is heard is the Christ within us, pointing out what we need to do. On the other hand, it may be an expression of the desire of our heart. In Kim's case, it was probably both.

STEP 9

SCRIPTURES AND AFFIRMATION FOR STEP 9

Life Principle: Being forgiving is to know forgiveness.

Read, meditate and journal on the following Scripture passages. There is one for each day of the week. Then use the corresponding affirmation as a daily reminder that going personally to the important other in our life is the best way to learn compassion and justice.

Luke 15:18-19 (11-24)	— I will take the initiative in making amends.
Ephesians 4:31-32	— To forgive is to be Christian.
Luke 6:36	— I will be compassionate as God is compassionate.
John 15:12	— Loving others is my goal.
Proverbs 28:23	— I will be straightforward and not talk in circles.
Mark 11:25	— I will forgive so I can experience forgiveness.
I John 4:7	— Loving involves doing loving things.

PRAYER

Jesus, help me to go to those with whom I need to make amends, so that I might learn true compassion and justice.

Amen.

STEP TEN

"We continue to take personal inventory and when we are wrong, promptly admit it, and when we are right, thank God for the guidance."[1]

Reclaiming our Lostness

Continuing to take a personal inventory is something that we need to do daily. Unless the 12 Steps for Christian Living become a lifestyle that we practice every day, they will not have meaning. Step 10 is a reminder that these steps are an ongoing process.

Because spiritual and emotional growth is a lifelong process, working this step is very important. As we evaluate our day — both what was "wrong" and what was "right" — we will continue to grow in self-awareness. Unless we evaluate, we cannot continue to grow.

By growing in self-consciousness we review what we have done during the day, evaluate why some things have not worked and why some have, and ask Christ to help us change what we can change. Through this daily evaluation, we may discover certain behaviors, which we are not ready to change, new destructive behavior may come to light, or we may learn and act on positive behaviors.

Perhaps the most significant outcome of working this step is the recognition and integration of our inner world with our behavior. *Webster's New Collegiate Dictionary* defines integration as "becoming whole."

[1]V. Bittner, *You Can Help With Your Healing,* p. 144.

This is what the Christian life is all about. This is the essence of salvation while we are on earth. This is finding the abundant life. Significantly, this is becoming what God created us to be. Becoming whole is the integration of our inner world with our outer world. It is allowing the Christ within to burst forth and become an expression of behavior that is Christ-like.

Integration is no easy process, nor is it without pain. Gaining awareness of the unrecognized and unknown parts of ourselves will force us to look at issues which are objectionable. Often these parts have been repressed because they were unwanted. Yet, these "lost" parts of ourselves must be unearthed, so that they can be redeemed and changed by the healing and transforming power of Christ to bring about wholeness.

However, as this step indicates, we also need to identify those strengths which have not yet been tapped. All of the positive, undeveloped parts of ourselves need to find a way to break forth in a legitimate way.

Most of us have so much of ourselves that is "unlived." Becoming what God wants us to be is exciting. Certainly most of us will never achieve our full potential, but life offers so much more than we presently have experienced. Working the 10th Step is one of the most creative ways of achieving our potential.

Our dreams are a means through which we are able to most effectively recognize the undeveloped side of our personality. That is why I have included dreams at the end of each chapter. The need to claim this unrecognized, undeveloped part of ourselves may emerge in a dream as a dream figure. For example, it might be a character in a dream who cries out for help.

The unlived life may also express itself as an inner turmoil of our personality. Inside, we may even feel as if we will burst, and perhaps we think we need to turn to something like exercise, drugs or some other "fix" to quell that rebellion. Unfortunately, this is sometimes the way that destructive attitudes which surface are momentarily stabilized.

This part of ourselves is asking to come alive. It is the unlived part of us, previously rejected and denied, which wants to break free.

Jesus speaks of this. His desire is to help us to reclaim the part of us which we have denied, so that we might be more whole and complete. He wants us to know the abundant life, and this will only happen when we have found wholeness through the integration of our outward behavior with our inner "Christ."

In Luke, Jesus says, "The Son of man has come to seek out and save what was lost" (Luke 19:10). Most Christians interpret this to mean that Christ came to save the people "out there." He came to save those other people who are lost and are not Christian. Without a doubt, Jesus did come to save all persons, to save whoever is lost to God. But the reference is also internal — Jesus came to save those who are Christian.

Jesus came as the perfect example of wholeness. He wanted to find and save all those parts of a person's personality which might be lost to consciousness, so that the person would be integrated and whole.

In the story of the lost coin in Luke 15:8-10, Jesus tells the parable of a woman who had ten silver coins, but she loses one and goes to great lengths to find the valuable coin which she lost. Without the one that was lost, what she has would not be complete, because the number ten symbolizes wholeness.

The lost coin here not only symbolizes the people who are lost to Christ, but also the parts of ourselves which need to be uncovered— both the inferior part and that part of our potential which we have not yet realized.

It is interesting that the woman "lights a lamp." In order to find that which is missing, we need to be enlightened, we need to be more conscious. We need to become aware of those hidden parts, the unconscious.

Probably the most significant part of the parable is that the coin is found in one's own "house." Symbolically, in the interpretation of dreams, a "house" is oneself. So, too, the house in this parable is ourselves. Therefore, the answer to who we are most often can be found within oneself.

Another interesting aspect of the parable is that she found the coin under the dirt. She sweeps "every nook and cranny until she finds it." The dirt here is perhaps our masks which cover up who we are throughout years of repression.

So to recover the lost coin is really to reclaim the lost parts of ourselves — to transform and redeem that which is negative and give freedom to the "Christ" within us to come forth. Then we can begin to reach our potential.

Jesus sums up the parable with the promise that God will rejoice "when one sinner repents." Jesus' goal is to help us find integration and wholeness. He is determined to accomplish this through the healing and transformation of our lives. This change takes place when we allow those hidden parts of ourselves to surface, so that they can be redeemed, utilized, and integrated.

Each of us has a stranger within us. Working the 10th Step can help us to reclaim that portion so we can start living the unlived part. When we reclaim it we will find salvation, healing and wholeness, here and eternally.

Goals by Which to Grow

As we work the 10th Step, we need some goals which will help us to evaluate our life and reclaim that which is unlived.

First, we need to work at *growth in self-esteem.* Perhaps this is the most important goal. Feeling positive about ourselves can help us to be more objective with ourselves and more fearless about uncovering those hidden parts. We need to remember: "I have called you by name; you are mine . . . you are precious in my eyes" (Isaiah 43:64).

When we uncover our weaknesses, we need not dwell on them. What we need to do is accept them, whether they are old behaviors or new awarenesses. If we embrace them and do not deny them, we can do something about them. We can change them, with Christ's help, or we can accept the knowledge that we are powerless over them and let go.

Second, we must stop destructive self-criticism. This is why we have added the phrase: "When we are right, thank God for His guidance." All other 12 Step programs have left out this phrase. It is one thing to give ourselves *constructive* criticism, and it is another thing to affirm ourselves because of the good that we do, thanking God for the guidance.

Most of us who call ourselves Christian have had a history of putting ourselves down. We have deluded ourselves into thinking that such action is synonymous with humility. Instead, it is being inhumane to ourselves.

Third, we need enriching relationships with others, not only with the important people in our life, but with those we know on a casual basis as well.

One of our basic needs as persons is to love and be loved. Some people do not understand, though, that this cannot be accomplished when we have a wall around us. We have to share love and give it to others; otherwise we won't receive it.

Steps 8 and 9 can help us in the process of developing good relationships. The key to having friends is a willingness to apologize and forgive. Unless we develop these positive attitudes, we will not have meaningful relationships. We must let go of the guilt and unforgiveness, so we will be freed up to be *with* others.

We must listen, so that we really hear what people are saying. When we don't listen, we need to admit it and be willing to change.

We need to be present for others. Whatever their need, we must be willing to do what we can and let go of what we cannot change.

We are to forgive . . . even "seventy times seven." Yet, we are not expected to put ourselves right back in the same old place and get hurt all over again. God respects us too much for this.

We will love without expectations. Having expectations without making them known is not helpful; we can only be disappointed. We have to risk loving with no strings attached, otherwise we will never know the joy which comes from loving freely.

Also, the only behavior that will attract others is following God's will for our life and praying that the spirit of His love will be poured out in our hearts.

Fourth, through the process of working the 10th Step we will hopefully reclaim the hidden parts of ourselves and come alive. We want to live our life with enthusiasm.

When we are enlivened with His redeeming power we will know His unconditional love and forgiveness and experience the joy of being creative. Then we can help others to reclaim their lives.

The key to finding enthusiasm for life is to take time alone to work Step 10. When we have difficulty being alone we will probably have difficulty being with others too. Solitude helps us to evaluate our life daily and also to redirect it. It also helps us to allow that hidden part to come out and to affirm what we find.

Fifth, we will work to reclaim our true self and allow others the same right. This means that we are open to this discovery and uncovering. It means that we are inner-directed and Christ-directed. It means integrating my inner self, both strengths and weaknesses, with Christ-like behavior.

This also means that I don't have to wear masks or play games, and I don't require others to do this either. When we are objective in our evaluation of ourselves, we will arrive at the point where we won't have to cover up, because we are accustomed to looking at ourselves honestly.

We are called to freedom — to be ourselves, and to let others be who they are.

Affirmation is Who I'm Becoming

Step 10 encourages us to give ourselves credit when we do things that are constructive, positive, and empowering for others and ourselves. The best way to do this is by affirming ourselves.

An affirmation is a method we use to achieve the goal which we desire for ourselves. When we affirm ourselves we see ourselves in the present, not in the past. We don't think of ourselves as we were. Rather, we see ourselves as the "new creation" which Christ is in the process of making. We focus on what God has done, is doing, and will do for us. We look to Him as One who is at work in us, doing "more than we ask or imagine" (Ephesians 3:20).

In a sense, then, our affirmations become prayers. We not only open ourselves to God's plan for us, but we affirm that He is already doing it for us. We affirm His promise in Matthew 7:7, "Ask, and you will be given what you ask for. Seek, and you will find. Knock, and the door will be opened."

In addition, when we affirm ourselves we need to use our imagination to visualize in our mind's eye what we are affirming.

When we image, we open ourselves up to the divine within. When we imagine, we are in the process of creating what we desire to happen. We are acting out the fact that we have hope in what we cannot see before us.

In Proverbs we read, "As a man thinks in his heart, so he is" (Proverbs 23:7). Even Paul tells us that we can be changed by changing our attitudes. "Be transformed by the renewal of your minds. . ." (Romans 12:2).

To know the will of God for our life, we must read His Word and allow it to speak to us. As the Spirit of God touches us, we are able to allow the "Christ" within to come forth, so we can be what He has called us to be. Our response to the Word is an affirmation, one which can be verbal or acted out.

To affirm God's promises for us is to choose what we will become. What we affirm now will be our future.

As we evaluate our life daily, and as we affirm what He has helped us to do today, we will discover that our thinking will change. We will be more positive, loving, and forgiving. We will be more Christ-like, because that is what His Word to us desires.

When we affirm what God has helped us to do on a daily basis, we need to read the Scripture for the day found at the end of each chapter. Next, we need to read out loud the corresponding affirmation. Then we image the affirmation in a way that applies practically to our lives.

Remember, imaging an affirmation is like planting a seed in the subconscious mind. It *will* bear fruit. Believe that! Don't disregard it. Remember, thoughts affirmed will grow into behavior, so we must make the right choices.

Life Example

Harris was struggling with a feeling that God had abandoned him. His wife was divorcing him. He felt as though his world was falling apart.

We talked about his need for forgiveness, how he had been forgiven by his wife for his controlling behavior. Yet, she chose not to live with that anymore.

That night he had a dream. In the dream he was a young

man, but he was dying of a heart attack. In his dream he actually died. After his death he felt his heart being replaced by one much bigger and stronger.

Harris had to die to his unforgiveness, so he could be born anew and be able to forgive.

The dream helped him to see that he needed to forgive God, even though his anger at God was illegitimate. He also needed to forgive his wife so he could forgive himself. He even began to realize how destructive his "hardness of heart" could be for him. He could have a heart attack.

As he talked more about the dream, he got in touch with another individual from his past whom he needed to forgive. In fact, his unwillingness to forgive this individual was the underlying reason for Harris' mistrust and unforgiving spirit, which had surfaced as a need to control.

STEP 10

SCRIPTURES AND AFFIRMATION FOR STEP 10

Life Principle: Live one day at a time.

Read, meditate and journal on the following Scripture passages. There is one for each day of the week. Then use the corresponding affirmation as a daily reminder that being willing to make amends is motivated by allowing our pain of guilt and unforgiveness to emerge.

Luke 15:8-10	— I will uncover the hidden parts.
Ephesians 2:10	— I have been created for good.
Galatians 2:19-21	— I have been "turned on" by Christ.
I Peter 2:16-17	— Freedom is a gift to be given away.
Matthew 7:7	— I am receiving because I am believing.
I Corinthians 7:23	— Christ has freed me.
Proverbs 23:7	— I will think positive and be positive.

PRAYER

Help me to grow in the discipline of a daily evaluation of my life, so that I will be able to integrate the "Christ within" with Christ-like behavior.

Amen.

STEP ELEVEN

"We seek, through prayer and meditation, to improve our conscious contact with Jesus Christ as we understand Him, praying for knowledge of His will for us and the power to carry that out."

Improving our Relationship with Christ

Having seen the value of taking a daily inventory, we then would concentrate on growing spiritually through prayer and meditation. *Prayer is really our affirmation that God's will becomes ours, and meditation is God's affirmation that His will would be ours.*

As we have worked the steps so far, we probably have had many spiritual experiences. We may think of a spiritual awakening which we speak about in Step 12 as a composite then of all our spiritual experiences. It certainly is this in part, but it is also based on the experience we have in the 11th Step. Working Step 11 is intended to help us "improve" our relationship "with Christ as we understand him." Therefore, Step 11 will help us to "prove" our ONENESS in Christ through the means of prayer and meditation.

What does this mean? In Matthew's Gospel Jesus summarizes the law and prophets when he says, "Whatever you want people to do to you, do this to them" (Matthew 7:12).

Paul reduces the two commandments of Christ to just one: "The whole of the law is summarized in a single command, 'Love your neighbor as yourself'" (Galatians 5:14). For Paul and for John, love of neighbor is the same as love of God (I Corinthians 8:1-3).

Thus, when we are loving and compassionate toward our neighbor, then we are one in Christ, and Christ is one in us. "If we love one another, God dwells in us" (I John 4:12).

However, not only are our compassion and love evidence that Christ is present in us and in others, but also that he is among us. When we are compassionate, we not only reach out to those around us, but we enter into the lives of others. We are connected to them, experiencing both their joy and sorrow, because the Spirit of Christ unites us.

His Will for Us

What is God's will for us? It is that His will would be ours, and that ours would be His.

How is this union of God's will and ours accomplished? It is through prayer and meditation.

How will we know that we possess the will of God? We will be loving and compassionate. Not only will we love others by being Christ-like, but we will see the Christ in our neighbor — even in our enemy. And we will know and radiate God's love revealed to us in Christ throughout His creation.

Therefore, Christ wills that we be compassionate and be examples of his all-encompassing love to our neighbors.

The Way is Difficult

Christ's way is opposed to all of society's values. The up-and-coming businesswomen and businessmen of the world often do not have Christ's standards. Being compassionate is not their goal in life. Many are empire builders who tend not to care how they reach the top. In fact, they often amass their money and power by walking on others, demonstrating a set of values in direct opposition to those Jesus intended for us.

Christianity is a way of life. So, too, is spirituality. The 12 Steps for Christian Living teaches a Christian way of life which is contrary to social ethics, or even *religion.* As we grow and "improve" our "contact with Christ" we will be able to discern the differences between religion and Christianity, and between the ethics of society and Christianity.

Being a Christian means that we are followers of Jesus. Being followers implies we are involved in a lifestyle. The 12 Steps for Christian Living provides a structure for this unique way of life.

A way of life and a religion do not convey the same meaning. In the Book of Acts, Christianity is referred to as "the way" (Acts 9:2 & 24:14). In the early church Christianity was never called a religion; it was called "the Way" — a way of life which emulates the life of Jesus.

Therefore, *spirituality* is a way of life. It is living our life as Jesus lived His. This is what a "spiritual awakening" is all about, and this is what the 12 Steps for Christian Living helps us to achieve.

The value of Step 11 lies in the help it gives us to improve our "contact," our relationships, and our oneness in Christ. This assistance is necessary if we are to be on "the way" toward a "spiritual awakening."

Christ's Way is an Attitude

Even in the Old Testament (Judaism) we are told, "You shall walk after the Lord your God. . ." (Deuteronomy 13:40). What does this mean? Are we to be God-like?

We are to be compassionate, as God is compassionate. His love for us shows us "the way" toward spirituality. Therefore, the act of walking God's way is being compassionate. Having compassion must become not only a part of our *conscious* existence, but of our *subconscious* life as well. It is to be an attitude toward life. It is not only a part of our thinking, it is something intuitive. We do it *without* thinking about doing it. It is an automatic response to life as we deal with ourselves and our neighbor.

Having compassion to the extent that it is an intuitive lifestyle means that we do not have to beat down our ego to be loving. Compassion flows naturally and freely, without any premeditated thinking.

When compassion becomes our spirituality, God's love is released. Then God's prayer for us is our prayer. As we meditate, we are able to hear God's prayer for us — that we be compassionate. This is His will for our lives.

In Luke 6:36, Jesus continues this emphasis, which is begun in the Old Testament. He says, "Be compassionate as your Father is compassionate."

All kinds of situations in the New Testament show us the compassion of Jesus — the experience of the two blind men who come to Him (Matthew 20:34), the leper who asks for a cure (Mark 1:40), the widow of Nain who lost a son (Luke 7:13ff). All of these illustrate not only the compassion of Jesus, but also the way in which people's pain moved Him to respond to them with love.

The people approached Jesus because they were seeking compassion; they had heard that they could find it in Him. For us today, as well as for them, Jesus becomes compassion incarnate; He is God's compassion made flesh.

Jesus' message to those who believe in Him and His Father, is a call to become compassionate. This call means, then, that being compassionate is a way of life, as well as an attitude toward life.

In Galatians 5:13-25, Paul identifies what it is "to walk in the spirit." In essence, it is to have compassion. This "walk" finds no place for the jealous and competitive spirit of the world.

The Value of God's Word

Prayer and meditation on God's Word will play a major role in helping us on "the way" toward an attitude of compassion. They will "improve" our "understanding" of God.

Knowing God as He is revealed to us in Christ is different from knowing a religion. To know and understand Christ and His love means, first and foremost, that we "walk the talk." We are to grow in our awareness of Christ and His ways so that we can walk the ways of compassion. Because Jesus is the incarnation of compassion, He then is the incarnation of this way, which we will emulate if we are His followers.

Being loving and compassionate implies learning an ethical system. It *is* being as much like God as is humanly possible. In a sense, Christ-like living involves others, but it is more than following a list of rules.

Christ came to "fulfill" the law, not to be the law. Therefore, being compassionate is more important than being ethical. It expands beyond ethics into a celebration of life. It is the best way we can honor our neighbor and our relationship with him.

Compassion is what "recovery" is all about. When we learn

love we have experienced a breakthrough between God and humanity. We have known a bit of what it is like to be created in the "image and likeness of God." We become a channel of God's love. Then we are able to share another's joy and bear another's sorrow.

When God created us, He gave each of us a portion of the divine. He breathed in each of us a part of His breath. Therefore, we are all sisters and brothers, because we are all children of one Father/Mother God.

Compassion unites love of God and love of neighbor. When we are really recovering and experiencing a "spiritual awakening," loving our neighbor is loving God. Thus, loving God means that we also love our neighbor. According to Jesus, the two are inseparable.

God's Word teaches us that knowing Christ is understanding love for God, others and ourselves. God's Word helps us to grow in "His will for us," and this is compassion.

We are not to be Perfect

Perfection is not what is meant by Christ-like living. If Christianity is to be our lifestyle, it involves our becoming *true* to the person God created us to be. This is the meaning of wholeness. When we integrate the "Christ" within and our behavior, it will become Christ-like, and we will know credibility, serenity, and salvation here on earth.

Compassion is the fullest experience of the spiritual life. It does not involve us in a quest to be perfect. Spirituality is walking in the path that Jesus walked. His concern for us is that we "might be one, Father, even as I am one in You and You are one in me" (John 17:21). The "one" implies that we become both one in mind and one in action. A oneness in compassion, but not in perfection.

We must not reduce spirituality to morality. (If we do, it is usually because we are feeling insecure and more in need of direction.) Yet, the integration of morality and spirituality is valuable to us. When we are growing in our spiritual life, our morality will become a way of living.

Then, when showing compassion becomes a subconscious action, as well as an action consciously chosen, it will be an intuitive act. And morality and spirituality will be one.

Christ's Gift of Power

As we grow in our awareness of God's compassion for us, we will feel the same for Him. "For the love of Christ controls us," Paul tells us (II Corinthians 5:14).

This is the key to our "growth in a new way of living." Once we have experienced the touch of the divine (compassion), we will desire to do nothing else but grow in our spirituality.

This motivation for spiritual growth and renewal is not something we have to do. When we experience Christ's love we won't be able to do anything else.

When I first became aware of the 12 Steps over thirty years ago, my first reaction was, "Who needs 12 steps to grow spiritually?" My pride was telling me that I was an intelligent person, therefore, I didn't need a bunch of steps to follow to find a closer walk with Christ. I was wrong! I *did* need it and I *do* need it. I need a structure for spiritual growth. It is true I did not need a lot of rules, but I did need direction for my life, because my life was unmanageable. If I had not swallowed my pride, I might still be without direction. As it has been said, "But for the grace of God, there go I."

The 12 Steps have helped enfold and keep me in the grace, love, and compassion of God. The more I know His compassion the more I want to know it. This is His wish for me, that I know His love and that I pass it on. Prayer and meditation are keys helping to unlock this awareness in me.

The more we trust the process of prayer and meditation, the more we experience His love for us. This builds our trust in Christ and empowers us to continue to work toward being the compassionate person He wants us to be.

When we know more fully His compassion for us, we are more willing to risk following the intuitive lifestyle inherent with the "Christ" within. Then, when our compassion is based on our intuition we are more willing to act on it because it comes naturally. We care and give of ourselves without thinking; compassion becomes an unconscious act.

Now, instead of acting unconsciously in ways that are destructive, we are acting positively, doing God's will for our life. We are compassionate — and it is "the way" we live our life. Compassion has become a lifestyle. This is spirituality and this is what Christianity was intended to be for human-kind. Christianity is not a religion, but a way of life which is like the way Jesus, through His example, taught us to live.

Christianity can become a lifestyle, if we are willing to work the 12 Steps for Christian Living. Then we will not only know that God is still in charge, but we will experience Him personally taking charge of our lives. This is a spiritual awakening.

Now we are ready to move on to Step 12.

Life Example

The dreamer in this dream sees herself in the mountains looking at some of the nearby cliffs. The high cliffs represent the place from which one could easily fall. The Apostle Paul reminds us that we need to be careful of this. "Let him who stand beware lest he fall" (I Corinthians 10:12).

The mountain, for Beverly, is symbolic of the fact that she might fall. This is something to be feared. The Bible tells us that it is a fearful thing "to fall into the hands of the living God."

But she decides to climb a neighboring cliff anyway. She is proud that she has conquered the mountain alone, without anyone's help, even God's. She finds herself sneering at the people below. They were afraid to climb, but she wasn't.

Suddenly, the cliff gives way beneath her and she falls into the valley below.

This dream seems to be a paradox. If she hadn't climbed the mountain, she would never have fallen, nor experienced the change which the fall brought to her life. It almost seems as though she had committed the sin of pride in order to be saved and know the love of Christ.

Paul asks, "Should we sin, so that grace may abound?" (Romans 6:1). The answer obviously is "No." Yet, at the same time, Paul is *almost* grateful for his own failures and hardships, because through them he has experienced the grace and compassion of God.

The dream, however, continued in an unusual way. As the cliff gives way, she feels she is being changed into a rock. A rock, for her, is an expression of that which is valueless.

Here she gains the awareness that she was incapable of realizing her own limits and mortality. To be able to see this she has to "climb the mountain by herself and fall down," disintegrating into a useless rock.

But then she hears a voice. It is as if the voice is coming from deep within her. She is pleading, "Jesus, Jesus, Jesus." With the sound of her voice, Beverly is resurrected. It is as though she has cried out in her compassion to the Christ who responds to her with compassion.

She has learned compassion, and she has experienced in a very dramatic way Christ's power in her life. He helps her realize His will for her life – that she would know compassion.

STEP 11

SCRIPTURES AND AFFIRMATIONS OF STEP 11

Life Principle: God isn't finished with me, yet.

Read, meditate, and journal on the following Scripture passages. There is one for each day of the week. Then use the corresponding affirmation as a daily reminder that God's will for my life is that I don't have to be perfect, but I do need to be compassionate.

Galatians 5:14	—	I will love myself and my neighbor.
Acts 9:2	—	Christianity is a way of life.
Galatians 5:13-25	—	I will walk in the spirit of compassion.
John 17:21	—	I am one with Christ.
II Corinthians 5:14	—	Christ's love gives me power.
Matthew 20:29-34	—	Jesus is my example of compassion.
Colossians 1:9	—	To pray is to understand the love of Christ.

PRAYER

You have shown us, by your example, your will for our lives. Help us to practice compassion with *others* and *ourselves.*

Amen.

STEP TWELVE

"Having experienced a new sense of spirituality as a result of these steps and realizing that this is a gift of God's grace, we are willing to share the message of Christ's love and forgiveness with others and to practice these principles for spiritual living in all our affairs."[1]

Basically, three factors can make working Step 12 very difficult: 1) we have not had a spiritual awakening, 2) we feel as though we don't know how to share God's love and forgiveness, 3) we fail to continue to work on our spirituality, not seeing it as a lifelong process.

A Spiritual Awakening

As previously stated, having a spiritual awakening means that we have begun to develop an intuitive lifestyle which is positive, loving, and forgiving. The primary characteristic is an attitude of compassion toward ourselves, others, and creation. This is spirituality.

This is also an awakening, because we have changed. We are now less negative, egocentric, and envious. We have become more in tune with the "Christ" within and the "Christ" in others. We also integrate our behavior to be more Christ-like.

In addition, becoming spiritually awakened means we move beyond dualism. Perhaps one of the most satanic lifestyles resulting from our compulsive, competitive society is the "either/or"

[1]V. Bittner, *You Can Help With Your Healing,* p. 144.

syndrome.

For this reason, in our 12 Step program we do not see character traits as "either/or," but as "both/and." In Steps 6 to 7 we do not use the word "*remove*." We use the words "*heal*" and "*transform*." As explained in these chapters, removing a character trait which is a weakness would also be removing a potential strength. A character trait must be viewed on a continuum. At one end it is a weakness, but when growth occurs it is primarily a strength.

Therefore, strengths and weaknesses cannot be looked at only from an "either/or" perspective. They must be viewed from the perspective that growth that has occurred in our lives. During our lifetime our goal as Christians is to transform our weaknesses into strengths, with Christ's help. This does not mean that the character traits will never be weaknesses again. Change does not happen overnight, and we do have a tendency to revert to old behavior when crises occur.

When we see reality as "both/and" we will discover the interconnectedness between our dark side and our light side. Unless we view life in this way we will not be able to be compassionate toward ourselves or others, nor will we be able to forgive or love. Without this perception of life we will not mature spiritually.

When we think about the Christian faith we realize it is "both/and." There is God who became human. This is the mystery of incarnation — the fact that Jesus is both divine and human.

There is grace, God's grace. This involves a story of humans becoming divine. Through the love and forgiveness revealed to us in the life of Jesus we are able to attain perfection. We are not perfect and will not be perfect by ourselves. Through the gracious act of Christ's death and resurrection we are forgiven and made perfect, we are made divine.

This way of thinking is called paradoxical. In Scripture we are told to "be in the world, but not of the world." Jesus tells us that "unless the seed first falls and dies it will not bear fruit," and also, "unless you (adults) turn and become like children you will not inherit the kingdom of heaven."

I am convinced that spirituality, a true spiritual awakening, cannot take place in our lives unless we change from being dualistic in our thinking to being paradoxical. Finding compassion and growth in a new way of living requires a new way of thinking, "both/and," not "either/or."

Until people have made this transitional journey they will continue to suffer from guilt and unforgiveness. Consequently, they will be unable to celebrate and enjoy life. They will miss the "gift of God's grace," His "love and forgiveness." As a result, they will have nothing to pass on because they will not have had a spiritual awakening.

Jesus tells us that only the truth will set us free. The truth states that we are paradoxical; therefore, we were created to be compassionate to ourselves, others, and God. We and the world are interconnected. We are "both/and," *not* "either/or."

Millions of people are slaves to trouble, environment and situation. What they want is to get away from it all. If they have unhappy marriages, they want divorces. If they don't like their jobs, they want new ones. They feel the solution is either/or. They are in bondage, because life is not that simplistic. The solution is usually found in a lifestyle that is "both/and."

Divorce is usually not the total solution. It may only perpetuate more problems. Getting a new job may be the best thing that ever happened, but it does not erase my weaknesses. Life that is mature must be lived as a paradox.

Thinking dualistically is the tyrant which must be overthrown before we can know freedom, that is, God's grace. If we are in bondage in marriages, jobs, or other human relationships, it is probably because we see our solutions as "either/or." Our slavery is due to our limited view of life. We need to accept that spirituality usually means growth through pain, not escape from pain.

Pass It On

In the 12 Steps for Christian Living we use the words "*are willing*" instead of "*try.*" It is true that we need to *try* to pass on what we have found through God's love and forgiveness, but we also must be *committed* to do the best we can. We must avoid making excuses for not passing on this message. As Step 12 states, we "are willing to share the message."

The key is "sharing" the message of God's grace. Sharing suggests compassion and caring, caring about the dignity of ourselves and others. The other 12 step programs use the word "*carry.*" The *Webster New Collegiate Dictionary* defines carry as "transmit to another." This implies that others need to be the receivers of our message.

In the 12 Steps for Christian Living the word is "*share,*" which indicates that we only *discuss* our views with them. Sharing is a dialogue and not a monologue. We are not involved in pressuring, controlling, or coercing others to believe what we believe. We are willing to tell our story without the expectation that others will believe as we do or live as we live. We are assertive enough to express our thoughts about the abundant life we have found in Christ, knowing that we can only help those who want help.

Perhaps the most convincing aspect of our sharing will be our *attitude*, not whether or not they *hear* our words. Remember the saying, "Enthusiasm is contagious." If we have really experienced forgiveness and reconciliation, we will convey an attitude of compassion and celebration. If our experience is only one of guilt and unforgiveness, we will subconsciously keep in motion a spiral of oppression, competition, and bondage.

When we have participated in the "gift of God's grace" we will know His "love and forgiveness." This awareness will be intuitively experienced by those with whom we are in dialogue. For forgiveness is one of the first gifts of God's grace which the Christian receives from the Holy Spirit.

How do we learn to pass it on? There is only one way — we must practice it by doing it. This is why small groups or meetings with one other person are so important. We can't do it alone. Healing does not occur in a vacuum. It occurs primarily in relationship with one or more persons who are committed to spiritual growth.

For example, the healing of pain is not achieved by the *avoidance* of it, but by *working* through the pain. The best way to work through the pain is with other(s). This is primarily through dialogue. When we share our pain with others, we not only face the reality of our pain and get it out, but we are in a better position to determine what we can do about it.

Therefore, through the process of healing our pain with Christ's help (dialogue), we have inadvertently learned how to share our story. We learned by doing it.

Practice It

We have determined that spirituality is a lifestyle. It is growing in living our life as Jesus lived His. It is also growing in our ability to forgive ourselves.

The most effective way to learn that God accepts both our weaknesses and our strengths is to remind ourselves of God's forgiveness. All we need to do is look around us and we will see God's goodness everywhere. God's creation is "good."

What has happened, though, is that all of creation has become corrupted by the destructive attitudes of humankind. Unless we accept this fact we will have difficulty celebrating life. We will get into "either/or" behavior and become unable to show compassion.

Jesus tells us we are to be compassionate, as God is compassionate (Luke 6:36). It is interesting that Jesus precedes this declaration with "love your enemies." Thus it is accurate to say that the biblical meaning of spirituality is not perfection, but compassion. Compassion is to be our lifestyle. The process of Christian maturity is growth toward compassion. This is the most complete expression of spiritual living.

The 12th step is vitally important for many reasons, but one of the most significant ones is that the key to spirituality is growth. As the step states, we are to "practice these principles for spiritual living in all of our affairs." Practicing these 12 Steps as a structure for spirituality will greatly enhance the possibility for growth. What we need to do is focus on ourselves.

We might like to change all sorts of people, but we can only change ourselves. When others hurt, we hurt with them. Our heart goes out to them, and we would like them to know peace. However, we will not be able to help anyone else achieve peace until we achieve peace within ourselves. And then we can only help them to help themselves.

As we embark on our own spiritual journey toward "growth in

a new way of living," we need to first become aware of our own spiritual vacuum. We need to conscientiously work on releasing destructive attitudes and replacing them with positive ones. This needs to be done on a daily basis, one day at a time, for the rest of our lives. I have found that the easiest way to let go of harmful attitudes is through the profound, yet simple program outlined here. If we are willing to follow these steps, we will be able to transform "the way" of Jesus into the way of life for ourselves.

When we view Christianity as a way of life we will experience growth through joy and pain as well as through sin and forgiveness.

For us, the important action is to "practice" these steps. They must become a way of life — otherwise the Christian faith will not become a way of life.

I know that one of the issues I keep struggling with is my need to keep growing. Sometimes I think to myself, "Haven't I grown enough?" The answer which continues to emerge is, "Yes, *but* God isn't done with you yet."

Growing spiritually is hard work. It is easy to rest on our laurels and convince ourselves that we have done enough growing. But none of us has arrived. We are all in the process — of becoming.

A good test as to whether we have arrived is to ask ourselves how compassionate we are. Most of us are still more compulsive than we are serene, and more addicted to something which fixes our feelings than we are at peace with ourselves. Thus *fear* is more at work in us than *trust*, and neurotic guilt (feeling guilty when we shouldn't feel guilty) uses more of our energy than the desire to expand spiritually.

If, however, we "practice" these Steps — work with them — we will grow, enjoying and benefiting from more effective relationships with others, God, and ourselves. We will expand our ability to be compassionate because fear will turn into trust, and self-doubt will turn into a willingness to grow and expand.

Nothing to Lose

Practicing these Steps also helps us to grow because they enable us to find freedom of the soul. I am convinced that true growth cannot exist unless we become willing to do anything it takes to be the person God created us to be. This growth begins with our willingness to face the darkness in our lives and see it as a potential strength, not a weakness. Growth begins when we reach the point where we have *nothing to lose*. Then, and only then, will we be motivated to grow. This entire process begins with Step 1, as we face up to our need for God.

If we have *something to lose* we probably will not be willing to "pull out all the stops" in order to grow. We must believe that nothing is more important than the truth and awareness we seek and the Christ we desire to be like.

Until healing and transformation are most important in our lives, we will not find the freedom to grow. Something will always hold us back. We must not have "anything to lose," otherwise we will lose our spirituality.

Spiritual growth usually only happens when we reach a "desert" in our life. Then we are ready to let go of all of the things that we thought were important, and focus on what gives meaning to life — compassion.

When we reach low points in our lives it is easier for us to experience Christ's healing in our lives. Then we are laid bare of our defenses and we are vulnerable enough for God to call forth the "Christ" within. By relinquishing control and giving it over to Christ, we are willing to allow God's truth to penetrate, so that we might know that compassion is the key to meaning in life. Then we will be able to be loving enough to "weep with those who weep and laugh with those who laugh" (Romans 12:15). And, in so doing, we will not only help others to help themselves, but we will also be able to relieve our own pain and celebrate our own joy. We will be enlivened to enjoy all of life.

Growth is not achieved by *adding* things to our lives; it is achieved by *subtracting*, by emptying ourselves. Spiritual growth begins with giving up and letting go. It begins with reaching the point in life when our humility and our willingness to admit to our need for God become the motivating forces. It comes when we arrive at the point where we have "nothing to lose." Then growth is a real possibility, because we feel energized to let go and take a new step of faith.

The "practice" of the 12 Steps helps us to face the reality of our "deserts" and our "darknesses." We are able to accept our need for salvation and reconciliation. We are able to be vulnerable enough to be emptied, so that we can be filled with God's love and practice more Christ-like living.

Thus, *we need to keep coming back to the point of having "nothing to lose."* This means we begin with Step 1 and continue on through Step 12. Otherwise, we will not continue to grow.

Spirituality is not achieved by doing more, or even adding more to life. It is achieved by taking away the things and activities that keep us from the freedom of having "nothing to lose." When working the 12 Steps becomes a way of life, we will find that we are free enough from the attachments of life to focus on our spiritual growth.

Life Example

Alex was having difficulty letting go of the resentment he had toward his father. During his childhood he was abused. He felt as though he could never measure up to his father's expectations. His father wanted him to be perfect.

I had given him an assignment to write a letter to his father, even though his father had died some years ago. I explained to him that this was a way to get the anger out so he hopefully would be able to release it. Then he could stop the control his father had over him through this anger.

That night he had a dream about his father. His father was dressed in a black robe like a priest. As his father came toward him in the dream, he was pointing an accusing finger at Alex. His father was condemning him for not being good enough. He told Alex that he wasn't any good, that he would never be any good.

In his dream, for the first time, Alex challenged his father. He said, "No, you are wrong! I am worthwhile because I am a child of God."

As we talked about the dream, Alex realized that the voice of his father had really become his own inner voice of self-doubt.

However, when he confronted his dark side, the side of him that said he was no good, he began to realize his own potential. When he realized his worth subconsciously, he began to actualize it in his behavior. He became more energized, confident, and assertive.

Alex's dream had not only confirmed the premise that one of his major issues was his father and his negative influence on his life, but the dream also revealed the solution. He had to face his father, thereby facing himself and his own opinion of himself.

His "desert" experience with his father helped him to become energized enough to work on his life. He realized that he had "nothing to lose" by working on his growth. This experience seemed to provide him with the freedom he needed to grow in his relationship with God. Now, for the first time, he was able to see God as loving, forgiving, and compassionate, so much so that he entered the seminary.

STEP 12

SCRIPTURES AND AFFIRMATIONS OF STEP XII

Life Principle:	I am only as spiritually deep as my story lets me be.
	Read, meditate, and journal on the following Scripture passages. There is one for each day of the week. Then use the corresponding affirmation as a daily reminder that spirituality is achieved through growth, and growing is best accomplished when we practice it as a way of life.

II Corinthians 1:3-4	— God's compassion helps me to be compassionate.
Luke 22:32	— Turning to God gives me power to tell my story.
Matthew 5:15-16	— I will be what God created me to be.
II Corinthians 3:4-6	— I know my value by Jesus' example.
Colossians 1:11	— I glory in God's strength.
I Timothy 4:15-16	— Growing is believing I have nothing to lose.
Hebrews 12:13	— I learn best by being an example.

PRAYER

Lord, give us the freedom from the attachments of life, so that we can approach spiritual growth with abandon.

Amen.

APPENDIX ONE

GROWTH IN A NEW WAY OF LIVING
4th Step Inventory Worksheet
by Joan R. Bittner

Step 4:

We make a searching and fearless moral inventory of ourselves — both our strengths and our weaknesses.

An important aid for self-awareness is the telling of our personal stories. This process involves remembering our past history and recalling the feelings and behaviors that resulted from the particular circumstances of our lives. In doing this we realize that we cannot change what is past, but unless we understand where we have been, we often continue self-defeating behavior and history tends to keep repeating itself.

Early authority messages/life scripts become habits that form the attitudes toward which we view all of life. These attitudes, whether positive or negative, manifest in character traits (assets and liabilities) by which we can identify ourselves today; for example, "Be perfect" manifests later compulsive behavior.

To begin the ". . .searching and fearless moral inventory. . ." you are invited to complete the following process of an honest, thoughtful and feeling walk through your life.

Suggested Preparation and Process:*

- Reread Chapter Four, *You Can Help With Your Healing,* and the corresponding material in the study guide.
- Have a notebook to write responses to the questions on the worksheet.
- Plan for some quiet time to relax and meditate on God's presence in your life.
- Pray for a return of life's memories.
- Expect to recall the scenarios from different periods of your life that will aid you in having a new awareness of yourself.
- Be confident that God is with you as you encounter difficulties.
- Be aware of distractions.
- Relax, and remember, "Easy does it."
- Pray Psalm 139.

"AN HONEST, THOUGHTFUL, AND FEELING WALK THROUGH LIFE"

I. Earliest Memories (3 – 6 years).
   A. Who are my parents? Mom/Dad?
   B. What is my homelife like?
   C. What kind of child am I? Describe.
   D. Earliest painful memory?
   E. Earliest happy memory?
   F. Any other memories of problems in earliest childhood years?
   G. Was I abused in any way?
   H. What 3 words would describe me at this time?
   I. What do others tell me about God?
   J. Other memories to note:

*You might want to repeat this process several times before beginning the 4th Step worksheet.

II. Grade School Years (6 – 13 years).
   A. How do I like school? How am I doing?
   B. What kind of child am I now? Describe.
   C. Any friends? Describe them.
   D. How are my relations with teachers and other authorities?
   E. How is my family life and home life now?
   F. Any memories of pain or problems during these years?
   G. Any sad memories of things done to me or that I did to others?
   H. Any sexual memories?
   I. Any exciting or happy memories?
   J. Any successes that I can remember?
   K. Describe religious formation/lack of it.
   L. What "messages/life scripts" do I remember?

Be good	Please others
Be strong	Be perfect
Don't cry	Work hard
Don't feel	Hurry up
	Other. . .

III. High School and College Years
   A. Where do I live and with whom?
   B. How do I like school? Describe areas of special interest/major.
   C. What kind of person am I? Describe.
   D. Any significant relationships? Describe.
   E. What kind of activities do I enjoy?
   F. How are my relations with faculty and other authorities?
   G. Any painful memories during these years?
   H. Any happy memories during these years?
   I. Any hurt, scared, guilty or resentful feelings? Describe.
   J. What are my values?
      - Do I live by them?
      - Any drinking/drug use? Describe.
      - What are my standards for sexual behavior?
   K. Any special successes I remember?
   L. Who is God?

- M. How would I describe myself at this time (assets and liabilities)?
- N. Other memories:

IV. Adult Years

- A. What kind of person am I now? Describe fully.
  - What are my values now?
  - How has my value system evolved?
  - What has been helpful in the process?
- B. Consider the quality of relationships.
  - What painful memories regarding relationships are there?
  - What pleasant memories?
  - Discuss significant others/marriage.
  - How is my home life now? Describe.
  - Do I work at improving my levels of communication with significant others?
- C. Discuss sexual life in adult years.
  - How do I meet my needs?
  - How do I relate to intimacy — both physical and emotional?
  - Any painful memories here?
- D. Are any children involved in my walk through life now?
  - I'll talk about my children:
    What are each of them like?
    Who is most like me?
    How is my relationship to them?
    Any painful memories of being a parent?
    Any successes or pleasant memories of being a parent?
- E. What is my work?
  - How do I feel about myself in my work?
  - How do I get along with others?
  - How do I handle any authority — employer, police and government officials?
  - Am I involved with my community/church? Describe.

F. Now I'll spend time on any painful adult memories.
   - Things I may have done physically, spiritually, or emotionally to injure anyone.
   - Things others may have done that injured me. Describe fully the feelings that resulted.

G. Has anyone close to me died? Have I experienced lost or broken relationships? Describe the grieving process.

H. Can I recall any life scripts that still rule my life?

I. I will think about addictive behaviors:

drinking/drugs	compulsive buying
sex	gambling
food	stealing
workaholism	destructive relationships
	other

J. Can I define what gives meaning to my life – my spirituality?

Now take a break and relax by meditating on Isaiah 43. To finish this part of the 4th Step inventory, I will list all the assets, strength, gifts and abilities I have. I will also list life's success. (This will take work and I may need the help of a significant other or group members).

Then, looking back over my personal story, I will write down the liabilities that seem to emerge, using the list on page 45 of *You Can Help With Your Healing,* and additional awarenesses that I have gained through other means.

At another time soon, I again relax, rest and meditate, and take one more walk through my life, again checking all the "lows" and "highs." Have I revealed all that is in me, all that I have done, or had done to me? Have I dealt with the feelings, painful or pleasant, surrounding all these events? If I have been open and honest throughout this 4th-Step adventure, I have begun to discover who I am and where I have been by recalling my life experiences. I am now ready for my 5th Step, using the 12 Steps for Christian Living as a guide.

Read II Corinthians 5:11-21.

APPENDIX TWO

STUDY GUIDE

1. Introduction

The purpose of the book, *12 Steps for Christian Living,* and the enclosed study guide is to help the 12 Steps for Christian Living come alive for all participants as a structure for spiritual growth.

2. Preparation

Getting ready for each session is essential if we are going to benefit fully from each group meeting. This isn't to say that it is not possible to gain from just participating in the group, but we gain most if we have spent at least 15 to 30 minutes each day in private preparation.

Preparatory study includes the following:

- *Read the chapter* in *12 Steps for Christian Living* before each session that corresponds to the step.
- *Journal on ideas* that are in the book that "touch" you.
- *Read and journal* on the "Life Examples" at the end of each chapter that speak to you. Dreams are used to encourage you to remember and record your own since they are a means for self-knowledge.
- *Post "Life Principle"* on a 3 x 5 inch card in a conspicuous location.
- At the end of the chapter *read the appropriate scripture for*

each day and journal on it.

- *Respond to the scripture with* the corresponding *affirmation,* remembering that an affirmation is a goal that I want to attain as a "new person in Christ."
- *Select a prayer partner* from the group to be your mentor and spiritual friend with whom you dialogue with on a regular basis, either by telephone or in person.
- *Pray the Prayer* or some other applicable prayer on a daily basis throughout the week.
- *Bring your journaling notebook* to the group for reference and for possible sharing with the group.

3. Reading of the 12 Steps for Christian Living

Each member in the circle reads one of the steps until all of the steps have been read aloud.

Twelve Steps for Christian Living

1. We admit our need for God's gift of salvation, that we are powerless over certain areas of our lives and that our lives are at times sinful and unmanageable.
2. We come to believe through the Holy Spirit that a power who came in the person of Jesus Christ and who is greater than ourselves can transform our weaknesses into strengths.
3. We make a decision to turn our will and our lives over to the care of Jesus Christ as we understand Him — hoping to understand Him more fully.
4. We make a searching and fearless moral inventory of ourselves — both our strengths and our weaknesses.
5. We admit to Christ, to ourselves, and to another human being the exact nature of our sins.
6. We become entirely ready to have Christ heal all of these defects of character that prevent us from having a more spiritual lifestyle.[1]
7. We humbly ask Christ to transform all of our shortcomings.[2]

[1,2]These steps have been revised from the original Twelve Steps for Christian Living found in *You Can Help with Your Healing.*

8. We make a list of all persons we have harmed and become willing to make amends to them all.
9. We make direct amends to such persons wherever possible, except when to do so would injure them or others.
10. We continue to take personal inventory and when we are wrong, promptly admit it, and when we are right, thank God for the guidance.
11. We seek through prayer and meditation to improve our conscious contact with Jesus Christ as we understand Him, praying for knowledge of His will for us and the power to carry that out.
12. Having experienced a new sense of spirituality as a result of these steps and realizing that this is a gift of God's grace, we are willing to share the message of Christ's love and forgiveness with others and to practice these principles for spiritual living in all our affairs.

4. Presentation and Discussion

The selected person will give a 5- to 10-minute presentation on what this step means to her/him based on private preparation during the week, as well as dialogue with her/his prayer partner.

Following the presentation, the group can break up into smaller groups (5-6 in a group) or remain in the larger group. This will be an opportunity for the rest of the participants to share their views about the step as it relates to their spiritual journey. The time allotted for this should be 45 minutes to an hour.

The recommendation is that each person remain faithful to the agreed upon step for the session. However, there can be exceptions. There will be times when someone will need or desire to talk about something that is on their heart. When this is necessary it is important to bend the rules. Yet, this person should be encouraged to seek out their prayer partner or another member of the group, rather than take the group off the anticipated step for the session.

5. Closing Prayer

After the small group discussion of the step as it applies to each of the participant's lives, the group convener should call all the people back together. If there is nothing that anyone wishes to share with the total group, the members need to be reminded of the importance of CONFIDENTIALITY, and see if the participants have any *prayer requests.*

One of the ways that the meeting could be concluded is by reading the following:

[1]In closing, it is important to remember that the opinions expressed here are those of the person who expressed them. What you have heard was spoken in confidence. Treat it as confidential by leaving it here in this room.

If you are visiting for the first time and feel that your concern or problem is worse than the others here, remember that everyone has problems, and there is probably someone else here who has a similar situation. Please keep an open mind. Transformation is possible for anyone who is willing to have Christ change his/her life.

Spend time daily preparing for the upcoming step presentation and discussion.

If you wish to call someone during the week, feel free to do that. Remember to spend one or two times this week talking to your selected partner or spouse. However, be confidential. Don't gossip or criticize. Instead, work at being understanding, and pray that the transforming love of Jesus might continue to work in your heart.

Finally, we need a volunteer to present her/his reflections on the ____________ Step for next week. Who would be willing to do this?

After reading this, the group could form a circle by holding hands. Then offer prayer for the particular requests, have the members pray as the spirit leads them, pray the prayer at the end of the chapter or some other formal prayer, and conclude with the Lord's prayer.

[1]V. Bittner, *Breaking Free* "Study Guide," p. 10

The Group Outline for Each Session

The following outline is suggested for the group experience:

1) *Opening Prayer*

This could be the Serenity Prayer, free-form prayer by one of the group members, or a written prayer that seems appropriate for the session.

2) *Group Purpose*

First, the convener could give each person an opportunity to introduce themselves and then read the following group process:

We came together in this setting to help each other grow through exploring and sharing feelings, thoughts, and values. We do not expect perfection from anyone. Rather, together we are to strive toward a more spiritual life in Christ. Hopefully, disabling aspects of character will be replaced by love, honesty, joy and serenity. The key for spiritual living is knowing ourselves honestly. Without this there will be no growth.

Each group needs one person to be responsible for leading the group through the phases of each meeting. The convener must discourage judgmental and critical attitudes and encourage sharing the gift of oneself and receiving the shared gifts of others.

All group members, including the convener, have a right to share feelings and thoughts openly, but no one should be domineering. What is shared in the session should not be discussed with others outside the group. The only person you are free to talk about outside the group is yourself. CONFIDENTIALITY IS ESSENTIAL FOR GROUPS LIKE THIS.

Yet it is certainly appropriate to contact others during the week between sessions, not for gossip, but for comfort and strength. Sometimes it helps just to have someone to listen to you.

As you come to know one another you might want to identify gifts in each other that could be useful in this and other groups — such as the gifts of leadership, organizing, intercessions, listening, discernment, teaching or spiritual direction.[1]

[1]"Study Guide Supplement" for *You Can Help With Your Healing,* Volume II, p. 1-2.

The Group Procedure

Spiritual growth requires two ingredients: a structure for growth, and a loving, accepting climate for personal sharing and dialogue. The 12 Steps for Christian Living groups provide this.

The group participants need to come, willing to risk TRUSTING the group *members* (even though they may not know them) as well as the *process.* They also need to come committed to being CONFIDENTIAL.

Participants need to come prepared to present their views on the step that is being discussed. *There is no right way* to give our presentation. It can be impromptu, prepared, or we can read from our journal. The most important thing is that we share our spiritual journey.

The Group Convener

This person is responsible for getting the group started with PRAYER, reading the GROUP PURPOSE, and initiating the PRESENTATION by one of the group members and the PARTICIPATION of each of the group members.

The convener needs to encourage all to participate in whatever way the person wishes. This is best accomplished if the convener is open enough to share her/his views. It is strongly recommended that participants share from the significant parts of their journal which they worked on during the week. *Remember,* no one person should dominate the group.

The Group Formation

The group can be organized when any two or three people want to grow spiritually and emotionally. The only requirement is a commitment to regular attendance and a desire to experience "Growth in A New Way of Living."

The usual time for each group meeting is 1½ hours. This study is best used as a *continuous study* in which it is repeated every 12 weeks. However, it can also be used as follows:

1) *Twelve-Week Study*
   This study would be twelve weeks in length or twelve sessions. Hopefully, after the first time through, the participants will see the value of repeating the process so that the steps become a lifestyle.
2) *Weekend Retreat*
   With this format all 12 steps would be covered at a weekend retreat.
3) *Individual Study*
   Using this method, the basic means of integration would be the journaling process.

APPENDIX THREE

GOOD GROUP EXPERIENCES DON'T JUST HAPPEN. They are the result of the commitment and involvement of the participants. We will be spending a number of hours together. May we, therefore, ask you to read, ponder and discuss the qualities of good group interchange listed below? And may we further ask you to adopt them in order that our time together may be fruitful, and a spirit of community and friendship may develop among us?

1. SHARING IS ESSENTIAL. Your thoughts, feelings and experiences are the life-stuff of this group. We all need them in order that insights may be discovered, understanding deepened and growth achieved.
2. Express FEELINGS, not just ideas. Feelings are the best indicator of what people value. To do this you must be in touch with your feelings. Take time to reflect on them and try to identify them clearly.
3. Expressing NEGATIVE FEELINGS can, on occasion, also be helpful. Unexpressed feelings simply set up blocks or dribble away in unproductive ways.
4. Respect, care about, SUPPORT EACH PERSON IN THE GROUP. The more confidence each feels, the more anxiety diminishes and the more deeply we can explore the topics before us.

5. SUPPORT NEEDS TO BE EXPRESSED. Don't presume that people somehow know you are feeling supportive. They won't, unless you show that you are. Hugs are Acceptable!
6. OUR GROUP GOAL IS NOT WINNING BUT GROWING. Don't water down your positions, but do state them in a way which allows people room for positive response.
7. Fruitful discussion requires OPENNESS TO CHANGE.
8. STICK TO THE POINT. Don't wander.
9. SPEAK FOR YOURSELF. Avoid using "we" when you mean "I." Don't speak for the group without giving others a chance to agree or disagree.
10. DON'T USE "I" SUBSTITUTES such as "one would think" or "any rational person would agree." Take responsibility for what you say.
11. MOSTLY SPEAK ABOUT YOURSELF. Growth occurs chiefly when the group applies the topic to their own lives.
12. HELP OTHERS EXPLORE AND DEVELOP the ideas and feelings they are expressing.
13. SAY IT IN THE GROUP. The things you say to your friends about the group before, after or between meetings are often the very things which should be said in the group. There should be only one conversation at a time going on in the group.
14. MAKE THE MEETINGS. If one person misses a meeting, the dynamics of the group change. And it often happens that the one who was absent cannot be brought up-to-date because he did not experience what really happened. The group needs to have you present.
15. ENJOY YOURSELVES. Life is too short to spend time doing things you don't like. Help others enjoy themselves by warmth, friendship and caring.
16. Above all — CONFIDENTIALITY is important. Whatever is said in the group must be kept in trust. The only one we can talk about outside the group is ourself.

Compiled by ICL Staff

APPENDIX FOUR

Opening Prayer

"God, grant me serenity to accept the things I cannot change, courage to change the things I can, and wisdom to know the different . . . living one day at a time, enjoying one moment at a time, accepting this sinful world as it is, not as I would have it, trusting that You will make all things right if I surrender to Your will, so that I may be reasonably happy in this life and supremely happy with You in the next."

Reinhold Neibuhr, 1943

Closing Prayer

Lord God,
make me an instrument of Your healing;
when I am weak and in pain, help me to rest;
when I am anxious, help me to wait;
when I am fearful, help me to trust;
when I am lonely, help me to love;
when I place You apart from me,
help me to know You are near.

Healing God, grant me not so much to demand everything from myself as to let others help me.

Grant me not so much to expect others to do what I can do for myself as to do my own part toward getting better.

Grant me not so much to seek escape, as to face myself and learn the depths of Your love.

For it is in being uncertain and not in control, that we find true faith, it is in stretching ourselves that we find our potential, it is in knowing the limits of mind and body that we find wholeness of spirit, and it is in passing through death that we find life and love that lasts forever.

Anonymous

NOTES

NOTES

NOTES

NOTES

NOTES